COSMIC!

EAST LONDON

Edited by
Jenny Edwards

First published in Great Britain in 1998 by
POETRY NOW YOUNG WRITERS
1-2 Wainman Road, Woodston,
Peterborough, PE2 7BU
Telephone (01733) 230748

All Rights Reserved

Copyright Contributors 1998

HB ISBN 0 75430 117 6
SB ISBN 0 75430 118 4

FOREWORD

With over 63,000 entries for this year's Cosmic competition, it has proved to be our most demanding editing year to date.

We were, however, helped immensely by the fantastic standard of entries we received, and, on behalf of the Young Writers team, thank you.

The Cosmic series is a tremendous reflection on the writing abilities of 8-11 year old children, and the teachers who have encouraged them must take a great deal of credit.

We hope that you enjoy reading *Cosmic East London* and that you are impressed with the variety of poems and style with which they are written, giving an insight into the minds of young children and what they think about the world today.

Contents

Avenue Primary School

Huma Ansari	1
Tahera Begum	1
Javed Patel	2
Shahara Khanom	2
Rahima Parwany	2
Nirali Patel	3
Shohana Rahman	3
Charanjit Lamba	4
Dharampal Singh	4
James Dennis	4
Karl Stewart-Miller	5
Nazira Begum	5
Shah Hussain	6
Summi Akthar	6
Alpesh Parmar	7
Shahana Bhanu	7
Shahed Chowdhury	8
Deborah Fabiyi	8
Fazal Uddin	9
Nadia Chowdhury	9
Fozea Iqbal	9
Farhana Begum	10
Tasneem Afinwala	10
Shahan Hye	11
Aqeel Mohammed	11
Tahir Patel	11
Nawal Jaward	12
Mizpah Lamptey	12
Saleha Begum	13
Shalim Ahmed	13
Prishant Roy	13
Safira Patel	14
Fatima Patel	14
Rowshonara Begum	15
Dilip Bhardwaj	16

Reena Kaur	16
Shamina Begum	17

Coppermill Primary School

Onur Uzun	17
Sarah Stapeley	18
Rosea Pickering	19
Mobeen Akhter	19
Chantelle Sinclair	20
Carly Lindsey	20
Stacey Aldridge	21
Lucy Green	21
Helen Davis	22
Sarah Edmonston	22
Jennifer Clarke	23
Laura Heffernan	23
Laura Riseley	24
Liam Cooper	24
Natasha McGhee	25
Laura Williams	25
Chantelle Raymond	26
Charlotte Goss	26
Lee Faint	27
Rani Sanghera-Warren	27
Paul Morrison	28
Alina Khalid	28
Yasin Akgun	29
Kristal Laskaris	30
Christopher Bingham	30
Dean Zammit	30
Courtenay Bayly	31
Sanaa Afzal	31
Liam Buckley	32
Christopher Bone	32
Darius Tingling	32
Joe Kearsey	33
Jamie Bursnell	33
Muazzam Chaudhri	34

	Matthew Slater	34
	Hinna Habib	35
	Hayley Taylor	35
	Mischa Wykurz	36
	Adeel Ahmed	36
	James Murchison	37
	Tayub Ahmed	37
	Kala Patel	38
	Zoe Buckley	38
	Tabassum Saboley	39
	Mohammed Fayyad	40
	Cassie White	40
	Nathan Grindley	41
	Chantel Brownbill	41
	Beth Kelly	42
	Saira Mahmood	42
	Billy Green	43
Davies Junior School		
	Faiyaz Patel	43
	Tia Ingram	44
	Asam Zaman	44
	Alisha McFarlane	45
	Irfan Farooqui	45
	Susannah Haynes	46
	Kirsty Louise Green	47
	Rajiv Patel	47
	Anna Rashid	48
Forest Prep School		
	Haniyyah Rashid	48
	Francesca Fox	49
	Devpal Bhachu	50
	Nicholas Bertenshaw	50
	Jamie Bajer	51
	Bryn Williams	51
	Chris Facey	52
	Alex Denham	52

Jack Keating	53
William Penney	53
Alex Levy	54
Matthew Fowler	55
George Murphy	55
Emma Oliver	56
James Dobias	56
Lucy Boggis	57
Pranav Bhanot	58
Aneet Baxi	58
Thomas Whittle	59
Michael Burgoyne	59
Sukhjit Bains	60
Georgina Lily Webb	60
Charlotte Harris	61
Katie Pickering	61
Victoria Rose Havercroft	62
Amie Kingsnorth	62
Laura Murray	63
Nisa Sekhon	64
Cristina Cooney	65
Laura Thorogood	66
Charlotte Elise Hall	66
Megan Greet	67
Janel Korhaliller	68
Georgina Leighton	68
Sarah Campbell	69
Abigail Evans	70
Melissa Kaye	70
Lucy Pottinger	71
Sophie Munday	72
Priya Malhotra	72
Stephanie Neary	73
Melanie Stevens	74
Elizabeth Pope	74
Hannah Whittle	75
Siobhan McElroy	76
Stephanie Moi	76

	Aiyna Singh	77
	Lauren Sewell	78
	Rosie Boggis	79
	Hemali Patel	79
	Sophia Vanezis	80
	Philippa Mansbridge	80
	Kirnjit Nijjer	81
	Katie Hulin	82
	Poppy Bristow	83

Gatehouse School

Katie Turner	83
James Paul Dale	84
Jason Marsham	84
Sheillee Shah	85
Gioksel Erzindjan	85
Mariam Nazir Banoo	86
Jay Donaldson	86
Emily King	87
Nisha Kumari Mehta	87
Roberta Makoni	88
Zain Butt	88
Jennet Lewis	89
Rowan Carreira	89
Zara Taraporvala	90
Hina Nazir	90
Jujhar Singh	91
Oliver Ingram	91
Marvin McLean	92
Gulsun Shevket	92
Nanci Lynch	93

Globe Primary School

Lisa Swaby	93
Cheryl Day	94
Lisa Merry	94
Maice Browne	94
Amran Hussain	95

Fatima Begum	95
Shahnaz Alim	96
Shujana Begum	96
Jabir Hussain	96
Barry Hanmore	97
Ryan Francois	97
Stacey Rolfe	97
Eric Duong	98
Gizem Uluozen	98
Shofada Khanom	98
Huma Yun	99

Grangewood Independent School

Amardip Marway	99
Marlon Regan	100
Harpal Bamrah	100
Liam O'Sullivan	101
Adaora Inyama	102
Cydney Loughrey	102
Ronell Rochester	103
Kiell Smith-Bynoe	104
Sannan Khan	104
Karen Sehmbi	105
Marcus Nurse	105
Shahid Zaman	106
Martin Eden	107
Danielle Roberts	108
James Harris	108
Esien Inyama	109
Charlie Fisher	110
Jolene Day	111
Jamie Fisher	112

Guardian Angels School

Rikki St John	113
Joy Knowles	114
Maxine Mullan	114
Laura Gray	115

Venus Urmatam	115
Donna Calleja	116
Tylishia Green	116
J J Facunla	117
Hayder Feely	117
Emmanuel Okorodudu	118
Steven Bush	118
Jack Curd	119
Aleishia Wilson	119
Emma Jayne Smiley	120
Antira Jones	120
Wayne Jones	121
Kirsty Shaw	121

Gwyn Jones Primary School

William Moore	122
Veronica Fayers	122
Shabana Buth	123
Shran Plaha	123
Melissa Wellings	124
Philomena Lines	124
Hannah Preedy	125
Ashur Lapompe	126
Amil Ourabah	126

Halley Primary School

Rahmin	127
Papiu	127
Kawsar Hussain	128
Juman Ali	128
Farha Nazmin	129
Ataur Rahman	129
Samina Lipi	130
Luke Pace	130

Harry Gosling School

Farzana Begum	131
Shajida Rahman	132

Shuba Begum	132
Nasreen Sultana	133
Shahidul Islam	134
Nilupa Yasmin	135
Jaheduz Zaman	136
Khaleda Hoque	136

London Fields Primary School

Hakim Abdul	137
Ella Flemyng	137
Joe Ngo	138
Leon Dunkley	138
Amy Williams	139

Nelson Primary School

Thomas Phillips	139
Kirsty Riches	140
Karan Murugavel	140
Sophia Charles	141
Sarah Main	141
Tina Muman	142
Daniel Pearce	142
Sean M Greene	143
Rejini Pradeepkumar	143
Raabia Laher	144
Farida Khanam	144
Siobhan O'Brien	145
Billy Evans	146
Lauren Champkins	147
Raminder Kaur	148

Olga Primary School

Lisa Perrett	148
Emma Brown	149
Charlotte Wright	149
Elizabeth Bollan	150
Claire Happe	150
Tom Kora	151

	Jamie Blanks	151
	Ian Coan & Ryan Wood	152
	Libby Sherman	152
	Sarah Oak	152
	Roxanna Spencer	153
	Debbie Lantsbury	153
	Ella Alder	154
	Stacey Burton	154
	Ria Joseph	155
	Laura Quinton	155
	Aklilu Teweldemedhin	156
	Aaron Jordan	156
	Holly Samson	157
Nightingale Primary School		
	Alexander Reid	157
Rushmore Primary School		
	Ola Akinrele	158
	Patrick Flowers	158
	Hinna Wadiwala	159
	Kieron Donovan	160
	Daniel Servante	160
	Ruby Silverlock	161
	Roxanne Apps	161
	Alice Barton	162
	Sophie Shnapp	163
St Agnes RC Primary School		
	Matthew Ting	164
	Charelle Modeste	164
	Jordan John	165
	Tendayi Jimbere	165
	Natalie Mathurin	166
	Dean Nevill	166
	Louise Leahy	167
	Paul Andrew	167
	Catherine Phillips	168

Kelly Welch	168
Iddanella Baumbast	169
Sam Watts	170
Natasha Lavery	171
Sean Griffin	171
Joanne Flaherty	172

St Antony's RC Junior School, Forest Gate

Neville Wandera	172
Jonathan Barquilla	173
Janet Castro	173
Karizza Torres	174
Laura Robinson	174
Amanda Rose Casela	175
Theresa Akintunde	176
Sarah-Louise Augustin	176
Ray Mierau	176
Bruno Camacho	177
Eva Owusu-Ansah	177
Lewis Iwu	178
Anna Vernon	178
Catherine Lovell	179
Leigh-Anne Defreitas	179
Jermaine Arthur	180
Nicole Smith	180
Jade Stanley	181
Cheryl Braganza	181
Munya Chidakwa	182
Alain Carver	182
Soraya Sackey	183
Isabelle Sarley	183
Hannah Gilligan	184
Amber Charles	184
Dawn Juckiewicz	184
Hannah Matthews	185
Michelle Browne	185
James McDonald	186
Quiana John Charles	186

Patrick Akintunde	187
Ryan Dench	187
Kristian Hamilton	187
Samantha Auguste	188
Rhian Joseph	188
Dwain Lucktung	189
Simone Dominique	189
Vanessa Laurent-Grant	190
Laeticia Bulambwe	190
Jennifer Flanagan	190
Simon Labonte	191
Antoinette Fontaine	191
Monique Clarke	192
Jonathan Loh	192
Heather Djan	192
Marvin Nicholas	193
Maria Cavilla	193
Zelda Prichard	193
Jonathan Peirce	194
Kehinde Oyegunle	194
Taiwo Oyegunle	195
Angelique Roccia	195
Leanne Vele	196
Nikal Jeyakumar	196

St Joseph's Convent School, Wanstead

Lucy Archibald	197
Melissa Fontaine	198
Hayley Wong	198
Katie Lim	199
Maria Coyne	200
Brooke Kirby	201
Francesca Le-Surf	202
Alison Fernett	203
Lily Elizabeth Jones	204
Victoria Jenna Jeffers	204
Luisa Anne Katie Bonomo	205
Samantha Coles	206

Olivia Jane Adshead	207
Clare Cubberley	208
Judy Frimpong	209
Sémone Modeste	210
Adjoa Anyimadu	211
Yogeeta Chandegra	212

St Luke's Primary School

Jo-Anna Mills	212
Charley Knight	213

St Paul's with St Michael's Primary School

Claire Rattigan	213
Deroy De Bordes	214
Grant Murphy	214

Salisbury Primary School

Claire Scoresby-Barrow	215
Kimberley Taylor	215
Adeeba Azam	216
Nazmin Begum	216
Vicky Patel	217
Farihaa Azam	217
Zahra Rammahi	218
Toni Goodwin	218

Shaftesbury Primary School

Saliha Khansia	219
Jigna Bhadresa	219
Raheen Saiyed	220
Mahjabin Choudhury	220
Wahidur Rahman	221
Sumera Saleem	221
Zaira Bashir	222
Rita Roy	222
Omran Tariq	223
Minesh Kanzaria	223
Sunny Pindoria	224

	Pritesh Sonigra	224
	Navinderpal Chana	225
	Aliya Khatun	226
	Neetha Kaur	226
	Mayuri Patel	227
	Sukhvinder Merway	227
	Sonia Bhatti	228
	Amena Umer & Amelia Chowdhury	229
	Usama Ihtasham	229
	Pritika Lal	230
	Hannah Zubir	230
	Kauser Hussein	231
	Karen Piekielniak	231
	Sayeeda Hossain	232
	Rajeepan Loganathan	232
	Viren Patel	233
	Arif Amin	233
	Zeeshan Syed	234
	Sabba Rashid	234
	Karen Johnsons	235
	Leona Campbell	236
	Tayub Nisar	236
	Alia Adam	237
	Reshma Halai	238
	Caroline Reilly	238
	Bharat Halai	239
	Hazera Begum	239
	Sunniya Mehmood	240
Storey Primary School		
	Claire Hastings	240
	Chantelle Drabble	241
	Peter Akinfenwa	241
	Liam Cesay	241
	Michael Parrish	242
	Lee-Ann Folagbade	242
	Egwolo Ekregbesi	243
	Christina Head	243

Anthony McCarthy	244
Alan Sanders	244
Deborah Anderson	245
Richard Henry	245
Stacey Donaldson	246
Carol Hastings	247

Wellington Primary School

Alexander Richards	248
Marc White	248
Daniella Hussein	249
Natalie Chalmers	249
Tony Braddick	250
Louise Britton	250
Darryl Neal	251
Nefise Dervish	251
Aaron Parvez	252
Timothy Gibson	252
Kate Newby	253
Aimée Swallow	254
Charlotte Barrett	254
Spencer Bain	255
Hayley White	256
Daniel Burt	257
Shakeel Sanghera	257
Karen Tapp	258
Hannah Bartlett	258
Terry Oliver	259
Bo Lauezzari	259
Mickayla Brown	260
Holly Sterling	261
Elysseos Odesseos	262
Kieran Street	263
Samantha Lustig	264
Christine Day	265
Karla Thurston	266
Lisa Clavey	267
Georgina Whitehead	268

Kerri-Leigh Jones	269
Joel Silverman	270

Whittingham Community Primary School

Heather Roffey	270
Stephanie Lashley	271
Nathan Onojaife	271
Calum Lewis	272
Joe Tollady	272
Hussnain Iqbal	272
Natalia Robinson	273
Amy Cantor	273
Nadine Gore	273
Loren Munroe-Thompson	274
Michaela Scott	274
Sahariyea Siddique	274
Zoyyah Imran	275
Tony Bradfield	275
Kyle Clarke	276
Ruebin Forbes	276

THE POEMS

BONFIRE NIGHT

The fireworks are zooming up like shooting stars,
The sky is light as if it was day,
The noise is as if a thousand lightnings have struck
When fireworks go off my heart jumps out of my body as if I've seen a ghost,
I feel like I have everything I wanted,
The people are pointing at the sky as if they can see the man on the moon,
The cats are jumping into their owners' houses as if World War Three has started,
The sky is raining with colours like a rainbow.

Huma Ansari (11)
Avenue Primary School

THE WORLD

The sun is like a bowl of pudding
for dessert.
The earth is as round as a ball
on the football pitch.
The sky is like a swimming pool with
clouds swimming in it.
A cloud is like a sheep with no legs.
The mountains are like a huge ice-cream
sundae melting as if it was snow.
The Atlantic Ocean is as cold as if you
were on the North Pole.

Tahera Begum (10)
Avenue Primary School

THE SUN

The sun is as yellow as butter
The sun is hotter than 10 million fires
The sun is like a lemon gleaming in the sky
The sun is like a balloon which would burst
in the evening and blow up in the morning
The sun is like a bowl of custard
floating in space.

Javed Patel (11)
Avenue Primary School

THE MOON

The moon is like a banana with no skin
The moon is like a white face smiling down at me
The moon is like a white balloon floating sadly around
The moon is glowing down at me as if I was on stage
The moon is as white as a dead person lying in the sky.

Shahara Khanom (10)
Avenue Primary School

POEM

The flowers are as colourful as a rainbow.
The moon is round like a face and shining
like a diamond in the sky.
The sun is like a ball of fire in the sky
which gives the earth light and heat.

Rahima Parwany (10)
Avenue Primary School

THE SUN

The sun is like a lemon growing
The sun is like a million billion light bulbs
The sun is like a daffodil
The sun is like a fire lighting on a cold
autumn day
The sun is like gold
The sun is like a million little gold rings
The sun is like a floating balloon in the sky
The sun is like a million hot ovens
The sun is like a billion houses
lighting up at night
The sun is as hot as a desert
The sun makes you warm like
you're sitting on a cooker.

Nirali Patel (11)
Avenue Primary School

A SILVER LAKE

A lake is like a mirror reflecting back to you.
A lake is like a silver carpet, silent and very
still and you feel like walking on it.
Sometimes a lake is very silent like no one else
exists on earth.
A lake is like a silver ribbon spread on the ground
sometimes it is straight and sometimes it is not.
A lake is like a huge silver coin, shiny bright
and silent.

Shohana Rahman (11)
Avenue Primary School

The Sun

The sun comes out in the morning like mustard coming out of the jar.
The sun looks like the burning desert sand.
The sun is as hot as an oven set on 'cook well'.
The sun's colour is as yellow as Liverpool's kit away from Anfield.
The sun is as bright as carnival lights.

Charanjit Lamba (11)
Avenue Primary School

The Sun

The sun is like a yellow hot balloon floating,
floating across the sky.
It looks like it is made of yellow butter
but I know it's brighter than a million light bulbs.
It looks like a big bowl of custard in the sky.

Dharampal Singh (11)
Avenue Primary School

Stars

A star is as bright as a silver ring
that somehow got stuck in the blackness of night.
A star is like the dazzling gleam of a diamond
stuck in the midnight sky.
The stars are like mirrors shining and reflecting
the sun's light.

James Dennis (10)
Avenue Primary School

BIG CATS

T he time is right to hunt
I have been waiting
G etting ready to hunt
E very tiger in my pack is hungry
R eady to pounce on my prey.

L icking my paws
I am waiting for the lioness to come back
O r come back with my food
N ow I am going to hunt my own food.

P uma is my name
U nderrated hunter
M eat is my food
A nd it could be you!

Karl Stewart-Miller (10)
Avenue Primary School

THE SUN

The sun is shining like gold.
The sun goes through the sky
like a balloon in the wind.
The sun is like a blob of
custard floating in the sky.
The sun is as bright as a sunflower
hanging from the sky.

Nazira Begum (10)
Avenue Primary School

EVACUATION

E vacuation is a sad time for children. They miss their family.
V ictory is a happy time.
A ir raid warden shouts, 'Light out.'
C hildren are sent to the countryside.
U nderground stations get shut down people go and settle down.
A ll men go to war to save their countryside from the Germans.
T rains were full of children going to the countryside.
I n the house people are getting under their shelter.
O ther people have no dad because they have to fight.
N ight-time is a dangerous time. Bombs fell on the ground.

Shah Hussain (11)
Avenue Primary School

WINTER CREEPS

Autumn is here time to harvest
Conkers are out children aren't about,
Then
Winter creeps, nature sleeps,
Birds are gone, flowers are none,
Fields are bare, bleak the air,
Leaves are shed all seems dead.

Summi Akthar (11)
Avenue Primary School

LIVERPOOL FOOTBALL CLUB

L iverpool v Juventus
I t's Fowler who takes the kick-off
V olleys it to Redknapp who makes an
E normous kick to McAteer
R ob Jones has received the ball
P aul Ince is clear
O yvind Leonhardsen has now got the ball, an
O verhead kick from him and
L iverpool are winning 1-0.

F owler snatches the ball off Zidane
O nly McManaman is outside the box, the
O pposition are not doing anything.
T he ball goes to McManaman. He
B lasts it and it's a goal
A nd the score is 2-0 to
L iverpool. Juventus haven't been playing very well
L ately.

C annarvaro with the ball and he
L eaves the ball to Inzaghi with an
U nbelievable shot and it's a save by Friedel. The whistle finally
B lows.

Alpesh Parmar (11)
Avenue Primary School

FIREWORKS

Fireworks look like the colours you work with to colour a picture.
Fireworks look like a fire being lit up by a person.
Fireworks look like the flash when you take a photo' from a camera.

Shahana Bhanu (11)
Avenue Primary School

DURING THE WAR

During the war what happened to me?
A bomb nearly fell and killed me.

During the war what happened to my Dad?
He went away to war to save our land.

During the war what happened to me?
I got sent to another country to fight for victory.

At the end of the war what happened to our land?
We killed the Germans to get back our land.

Shahed Chowdhury (10)
Avenue Primary School

THE SUN

The sun is like a fireball in the sky
The sun shines like a plate of gold.
The sun is like a yellow wheel falling across the blue sky.
If you go too near the sun it would sound just like someone was
 lighting lots of jets on a gas cooker.
If I could get close enough (not to burn) just to smell I think it would
 smell like a great juicy orange that someone just peeled.

Deborah Fabiyi (11)
Avenue Primary School

WEATHER

It's raining, it's pouring, it's snowing, it's foggy, it's gloomy,
      it's muddy the flowers are dying.
The leaves are falling
The car is wet. The windows are wet.
The sun is coming out. The rain is going.
The flowers are growing. The leaves are not falling.
It's breeze. It's blizzard. It's ice.

Fazal Uddin (11)
Avenue Primary School

THE CLOUDS

The clouds are like fluffy feathers or like candyfloss flying
      across the sky.
They are big and fluffy and white as snow.
Sometimes they look like ghosts high above me.
They look like sheep walking in the sky.
The clouds look like big bunches of white flowers.

Nadia Chowdhury (11)
Avenue Primary School

BLACK AND PURPLE

The colour of darkness Halloween,
When the witches fly by wearing black and purple.
Reminding me of graveyards,
Fear of blackness,
Darkness.

Fozea Iqbal (11)
Avenue Primary School

A New Spell

Horror, horror
Let's make a new spell
Put in some dead mice
with some green dice,
stir, stir, stir
horror, horror.
Put in some old books
with some dirty hooks,
stir, stir, stir,
horror, horror.
Put in some fat rats
with some ugly bats,
stir, stir, stir.
Now it's finished.
Open wide, gulp, gulp!
Ha, ha, ha.

Farhana Begum (11)
Avenue Primary School

Relaxation

Relaxation is bright turquoise,
warm as the Caribbean sea.
Its taste is like sweet sugar
and honey fighting all the sour bits
It sounds like a violin singing
through the cool air.
It smells like a fresh
bright rose.
It feels as soft as the clouds.

Tasneem Afinwala (10)
Avenue Primary School

WHAT AM I?

I am very big
With a very long nose
I have four fat feet
And very large ears
To keep me cool
What am I?

Shahan Hye (8)
Avenue Primary School

ANGER

Anger is red and orange.
It sounds like an earthquake.
It could blast open your head.
It makes people scared.
It makes them run away.

Aqeel Mohammed (11)
Avenue Primary School

MOVING

Letting out my long tongue
Twisting and twirling wherever I go
Hissing whenever I move
Sliding on tree branches.

Tahir Patel
Avenue Primary School

Left Out

No one looks like they're my friend
I am always the one who's left out
Whenever I give ideas
People usually don't agree
Whenever I am upset
They don't even care
Every time I want to speak to them
They always walk away
I always feel lonely and friendless
Even though I want to be their friend
They always walk away
Whenever I am lonely
This is what makes me feel better
I write it down on paper
Or speak to someone about my feelings.

Nawal Jaward (11)
Avenue Primary School

Excitement

Excitement feels as gentle as the clouds.
Its favourite colour is bright orange with sunny spells of yellow.
Excitement resembles an eagle with feathers that are all the colours
                                                            of the world.
It tastes like strawberry gateau and flavours of fruit in one bubblegum.
Excitement sounds like an orchestra playing Beethoven
The fragrance smells like a chest of gold with sunflowers, bluebells
                                                    and daffodils.

Mizpah Lamptey (11)
Avenue Primary School

ANGER

Your face goes red, erupting lava coming out,
It's like hot red blood being boiled in a pan.
Your nose feels blocked because there's no space to breathe,
While your face is full of anger.
Your body is steaming like a metal machine going down your spine.
Your brain can't control your anger but the rest of your mind
                                            starts to cool down.

Saleha Begum (10)
Avenue Primary School

ELEPHANTS

Elephants are big and fat.
Need to eat all the time.
They have big trunks and weigh a ton.
They have big wrinkly bodies but small bushy tails.
They have big white tusks.
They have big fat legs.
They flap their big ears when happy.

Shalim Ahmed (11)
Avenue Primary School

ANGER

Anger
Anger is a bad flame
Anger is red-hot blood
Everyone gets angry
I feel like strangling someone.

Prishant Roy (10)
Avenue Primary School

SAYING GOODBYE

Goodbye Grandfather
I don't know what to say.
What can I say?
There will always be a place
in my heart for you and I
will never forget you.
My heart is torn apart and
I will remember all the good
times we had and I will
remember the stories you told me.
Grandfather I will remember
you today and every day
Love Safira.

Safira Patel (10)
Avenue Primary School

JOY

Joy is bright yellow.
It shines through your bedroom window
and that's when your joy begins.
It sounds like someone playing a guitar with mirth.
It feels like soft wet sand on the beach.
It smells like honey and sweetness around you.
It tastes like fresh mint inside your heart.

Fatima Patel (11)
Avenue Primary School

SEASONS

The wind is cold
The clouds are blue
When snow is here
It freezes my ears.

People in the world
Are cold and hot
But when summer is here
Everyone's hot.

When autumn is here
Leaves turn brown and orange
And fall off trees
Children throw leaves around the streets
And have lots of fun.

Boys and girls pick conkers
From trees in the park
They throw them, they kick them
They play conker fights.

When spring is here birds sing
They get ready to settle
And make their nests.

Rowshonara Begum (11)
Avenue Primary School

END OF EARTH

Comet!
People shout and scream loudly
Big planets break up from planets,
Loud noises with red-hot big stones
Going very fast,
Red flames shooting
Bang!
Earth is destroyed
Parts of Earth vanish in mid air
It is dark
Small rocks float in the air
It's really hot
Silence.

Dilip Bhardwaj (10)
Avenue Primary School

MY WORRIES!

I like to think of nice things
But all my worries come along.
I want my worries to disappear
I don't know if I am right
I don't know if I am wrong.
I don't know about the good things
I've done to be good
I would like to clean my feelings off
Because I feel alone, alone, alone.

Reena Kaur (10)
Avenue Primary School

ALL ON MY OWN

I feel so depressed
No one is here for me
No one cares for me
I am like a very lonely person
Sitting in the middle of the room
When I go to sleep all I dream of is my family
I go downstairs and hear a knock on the door
I run but it's never them
So my heart starts beating
My eyes start going red
When my tears start dropping.

Shamina Begum (11)
Avenue Primary School

THE STORM

Wind, lightning, thunder and rain, destroying houses and trees.
I am so scared, please save me.
Animals in fear run for their lives.
Plants and grass get too much water,
If the storm won't stop it will cause a disaster.
Stray cats and dogs running around everywhere.
The storm is so cold, I nearly feel bare.
I hope the sun will come out, then we will be happy,
Please sun come out,
The storm will then go and the animals will play about.

Onur Uzun (11)
Coppermill Primary School

UNDER THE SEA

Under the sea,
A place for me,
Here comes a shark,
It's playing like 'he' in a park.

Down deep in the sea,
There's a city,
Anchovies eating pizza,
Tunas playing trombones,
Crabs watching casually.

Down deep in the heart of the city,
A beautiful princess sea-horse.

Another part of the sea
Has different animals.

Up on the surface of the sea
Dolphins play away,
Rolling over,
Breaking the sun of the up top sea,
Jumping, spinning in the sea.

Under the sea, a place for me,
Here comes a shark, got to run,
It's not all fun,

Under the sea!

Sarah Stapeley (10)
Coppermill Primary School

CHOCOLATE

Smooth taste,
Chocolate melts in your mouth,
Piece after piece,
Like heaven,
Each piece, fragile, delicate.
The smell and taste,
So delightful, as though there is no better taste,
Luxurious,
Taste takes you away,
Somewhere where you can enjoy,
The tantalising relish
Of chocolate.

Rosea Pickering (11)
Coppermill Primary School

MY FAVOURITE THINGS

Big
Hairy
Brown wet nose
Pink mouth
Big, fat, eyes brown
Squishy nose, thick mouth
Little arms, little feet
Walks on two legs
It's a teddy bear!

Mobeen Akhter (8)
Coppermill Primary School

IN THE DARK BED

When I'm in the dark in bed
I look around to see things

When I'm in the dark in bed
I think about ghosts, creepy ghosts

When I'm in the dark in bed
I twist and turn to get warm

When I'm in the dark in bed
I make pictures with my eyes

When I'm in the dark in bed
I close my eyes and sleep.

Chantelle Sinclair (10)
Coppermill Primary School

HOME AT LAST

Through the cold, I run home from school,
To see my mum all snug and warm,
She runs me a bath with bubbles too!
Mum takes my temperature, I have the flu.
I come out of the bath all warm again,
Mum reads me a story about snowmen.
As I doze off my eyes closing fast
I think to myself, I'm home at last.

Carly Lindsey (10)
Coppermill Primary School

SCHOOL LIFE

School Dinners

Ugly dinners are vile,
grumpy cook who is ratty,
dinners with a strange mixture, peas and carrots everywhere.
They are yucky, nothing we like,
dreadful custard.

After In The Playground:

Tyrannical midday's,
always giving us grief,
never stop telling us off,
some are helpful and kind.
Groany bad boys playing football,
horrible bullies who we don't like.
Girls giggling about boys,
smelly stinky toilets, but I've got to go.
Jumpy joyful children playing skipping,
kind children looking after each other.

Stacey Aldridge (9)
Coppermill Primary School

GO TO BED

Come on Zoe, go to bed,
Please Zoe go to bed
You need to go to school tomorrow
Zoe please, I need you to go to bed,
I need to go to work tomorrow
Just please go to sleep.

Lucy Green (10)
Coppermill Primary School

SWIMMING

Once a week, I go swimming with my dad,
When walking into the swimming pool and I can only smell chlorine
I hurry to get ready, pushing my hair into my cap.
Suddenly, everything goes quiet,
Down the stairs I run to give my big, heavy bag to my dad,
Waiting to be called for my class, shivering a bit
Partly from the cold, partly from all of the excitement.
Called by the teacher to the pool we have to get straight in,
Feeling as though I am a snake slithering down a steep hole.
I felt as though I was a mermaid swimming to the shore when I race
                                                                with my friends.
Up and down we swim passing one another like a flash,
When the lesson is over we all get out wet and shiny
Going to get our swimming bags to get changed
The swimming costume feels like an elastic band
Because it is so tight around my waist.
Rushing to get changed and drying my dripping hair
Quickly going down stairs to my dad and we go home.

Helen Davis (10)
Coppermill Primary School

ON THE WAY TO THE BUS STOP

I'm walking down this same old street,
Listening to the tip tap of my feet.
The icy winds are chilling me to the bone,
Whilst I'm sitting at this bus stop all alone.
The wind is as cutting as a splinter,
Why must I do this in the middle of winter?

Sarah Edmonston (10)
Coppermill Primary School

MY FAVOURITE THING

My favourite thing . . .
Is white and furry . . .
He is smaller than a hand
He has a little pink nose,
He climbs on his cage
He is very funny
He likes to do his gym in a hurry
It likes to eat cucumber and biscuits as a treat
My favourite thing is . . .
My sweet little hamster
I know this will make you laugh his name is Meatball
I didn't choose that name my brother did.

Jennifer Clarke (8)
Coppermill Primary School

PARADISE ISLAND

Tropical palm trees swaying in the moonlight,
Clear ocean water with dolphins leaping with joy and playing.
Deadly sharks waiting for their prey,
Glittering stars up above, the moon shining on the ocean.
The cool, smooth air flapping in your face
As you float along the warm ocean
Lovely, smooth, hot sand.

Laura Heffernan (10)
Coppermill Primary School

PETS AND RELATIVES DON'T GO!

I had a little puppy,
As cute as can be,
I showed him to my parents,
Who ate him up for tea.

I had a furry pussy cat,
Purring at my feet,
I showed him to my brother,
Who chopped him up for meat.

I had a shiny goldfish,
Swimming in the sun
I showed him to my grandma,
Who shot him with her gun.

Laura Riseley (10)
Coppermill Primary School

THE COW THAT LOVED TO CHEW

There once was a cow that loved to chew.
He loved to chew gum and Wrigley's spearmint too.
He chewed and chewed until one night
When the moon shone really bright,
The cow found, that he couldn't chew or bite.
His teeth had fallen out in the night, so he stuck them in, with
                                            superglue in fright.
There once was a cow that loved to chew
He liked to chew gum and Wrigley's spearmint too.

Liam Cooper (11)
Coppermill Primary School

LOOKING OUT OF MY WINDOW

Looking out of my window,
I see different kinds of plants.
All of them starting to bloom.
All of them bright, different colours,
Colours of: oranges,
Reds,
Yellows,
Blues,
Pinks and many more.
I see different kinds of animals,
All fascinating to see,
Animals like speedy foxes,
Furry cats,
Tiny insects and many more.
I see different kinds of buildings,
All different shapes
Shaped long,
Short
Squared and many more.
Looking out of my window,
I see a different life.

Natasha McGhee (11)
Coppermill Primary School

THE WIND IS A HOUND

The wind is a hound,
Howling through the night,
Rain dripping from its mouth
Snapping branches in half as it darts here and there.

Laura Williams (9)
Coppermill Primary School

IF I WAS IN A DEEP BLUE SEA

If I was in a deep blue sea
Nights as dark as they could be
Turn my head and look and see
If a shark is after me.
The thing that I would like to be
Is a mermaid or a fish maybe
A coral sinking down and down
But not a shark that makes a sound.
If I was out of that big sea
I'd be my normal self that's me
I'd look around and go to bed
Without a single word being said.

Chantelle Raymond (10)
Coppermill Primary School

THE BLACK CAT

It hangs around the corner,
Stalking its prey,
Watching its every move.
His jet black fur vanishes into the darkness,
Camouflaged by the forest of evil.
He makes the pounce,
The eight daggers stick out,
As he digs them into his prey.
The black cat strikes again.

Charlotte Goss (10)
Coppermill Primary School

SUMMERTIME

The sky is blue,
The cows go moo.

The grass is green,
Where has the sun been?

Tucked away on winter days,
Now it shines, hip, hip, hooray!

The days are long and bright,
Lollies, ice-creams, what a sight!

Laughter, joy and happy faces,
Busy, visiting sunny places.

Lee Faint (10)
Coppermill Primary School

MY FAVOURITE THING

Small
White
Eats carrots
Runs all over the garden
Has long ears
Lives in a hutch
Has a friend called Baba
Has sharp claws
I think it is lovely
When I pick her up
She is nice and fluffy.

Rani Sanghera-Warren (7)
Coppermill Primary School

THE JUNGLE

The jungle with all of its tropical colours,
Beautiful birds flying around in the air,
Looking for fruit, succulent and juicy.
Toucans squawking their noisy songs,
Snakes coiling around a branch,
Their tongues finding their prey,
Hunters hunting the animals' tracks along the ground,
Unlucky for them - they do not catch anything!
The animals are too crafty for them.
The insects buzzing around,
Annoying the animals,
Squelched to the ground!
Pretty flowers all around,
The smell is a perfume rare,
Which you can't find anywhere.

Paul Morrison (11)
Coppermill Primary School

MY FAVOURITE THING

It's small.
It's white.
It's furry.
It's got a fluffy tail.
It is fat.
It eats currants.
It jumps around.
My favourite thing is a rabbit.
My rabbit's name is Tom.

Alina Khalid (8)
Coppermill Primary School

THE COMPUTER AGE

Where would we be?
If only we knew.
The computer is here,
It helps us go through.

Our learning is aided
By buttons and mice,
We move it around
To make our work nice.

And then came along,
The new CD Rom.
Goodbye floppy discs,
Hello 3-D song.

A sound card is needed
To keep it ablast,
Are we going mad?
We've moved on from the past!

Everything's high-tech and Pentium 2
PCs and Laptops are far from few.
Money is no big deal
In a world with not much feel.
The virus is here
There seems a need to steal.

Information on the Internet!
A new sport is here.
Surfing the net
Without even getting wet,
What a wonderful deal!

Yasin Akgun (11)
Coppermill Primary School

My Favourite Thing

Fluffy and round
Small brown eyes
Wet paw-prints
Likes chocolate buttons
Plays with you
Wags her tail
I think she is cute.

Kristal Laskaris (8)
Coppermill Primary School

My Favourite Things

Shine in the moonlight
Lights in the sky
Shaped with triangles
Shining bright in the sky
I cannot count them
In the moonlit sky.

Christopher Bingham (7)
Coppermill Primary School

My Favourite Thing

Small,
Naughty,
His is a little rascal,
He sleeps in my room,
He is very funny,
Sometimes he is stinky.

Dean Zammit (7)
Coppermill Primary School

MY FAVOURITE THING

Tiny
White
Furry
Little pink tail
Wriggles like mad
Walks quite fast
Runs away in a ball
Loads of energy
Hides behind the sofa
The little rascal gets away when you come near
Guzzles food stored in cheeks.
Loves lettuce
My tiny pet gets lost
I find him again
(It is a hamster!)

Courtenay Bayly (8)
Coppermill Primary School

MY FAVOURITE THING

Big
fluffy ears
brown
big black nose
big round eyes
big mouth
nice big smile.
It smiles all the time
It's hairy
It sleeps on my bed.
Lots of energy
It's my teddy bear.

Sanaa Afzal (8)
Coppermill Primary School

MY FAVOURITE THINGS

It's fast like a rocket
It goes broom, broom
It's very fast, really fast
It is really thin
It is double plated
And when the sun shines
It shines back.

Liam Buckley
Coppermill Primary School

MY FAVOURITE THING

Black and white,
Small,
Eats fish,
Sleeps on my bed,
Loves the fire,
Hates water,
Chases mice and rats.

Christopher Bone (7)
Coppermill Primary School

FUN

Playing games is what I love to do
When the sun is shining and the sky is blue,
But even when there's wind and pouring rain
That will not stop me, I'll not refrain.
Because even then I will kick a ball, jump, skip or even run.
But most of all I'll have fun, fun, fun!

Darius Tingling (10)
Coppermill Primary School

SCHOOL POEM

Fantastic swimming
children splashing
trying your best and
working hard.
Falling under water
jumping in cold pool.
Kind teacher because she
does not shout.
Falling under and water going
up your nose.
Lost 50p in the lockers,
trying to get ready first.
Can't wait for fun day,
can't wait to dive,
can't wait to go home,
can't wait to sleep.

Joe Kearsey (9)
Coppermill Primary School

SCHOOL POEM

My mum's best friend is a supply teacher.
 She smokes a lot, I wonder why?
When she is on duty she lets
 us have a longer playtime.
She always gives us easy English work.
 She always gives us messy art work.
She always gives us really hard maths work.
 I wish she was here every day.

Jamie Bursnell (10)
Coppermill Primary School

SCHOOL POEM

Teachers grumbling whenever they get a chance.
Screeching chairs as miserable children get up.
Masterful teachers, which they are not.
Teachers aggravating children to do bad things.
Clock ticking as teachers moan.
Bad-tempered teachers as usual.
Hardly any helpful staff.
Flabby teachers make the ground tremble.
Library's full of fascinating book.
Tedious routines like looking up spellings.
Children never giving teachers grief.
Assemblies always enjoyable.

Muazzam Chaudhri (9)
Coppermill Primary School

WARNING FIVE-YEAR-OLDS TO TEN-YEAR-OLDS ONLY!

Dull maths, endless work,
Hours of boring science, silly English,
Brilliant art but not much of it,
Spelling test, tables test, 'Absolute silence now!'
It's like a prison cell with all that quietness,
Hard homework, wish we didn't have work,
Especially homework and handwriting.
I nearly had a nightmare about homework,
So remember don't work too hard
Because you'll end up like me.

Matthew Slater (10)
Coppermill Primary School

ART POEM

Have to roll sleeves up.
Have to put newspaper out.
Have to wear an apron.
Tremendous when squirting on paper.
Flinging paint all over clothes and hands.
Playing with paint.
Fun mixing colours.
Making a jumble everywhere.
Tossing water when doing washing up.
Art is great!

Hinna Habib (10)
Coppermill Primary School

SCHOOL POEM

The yellow line
is bright like the sun,
And the green
is the growing grass,
The blue is like the ocean
proud and free.
All the different paint colours
on the playground floor,
that's why I like playtime.
Why can't they bring the
colours inside?

Hayley Taylor (10)
Coppermill Primary School

MATHS

Maths is too easy, needs to be harder.
Sometimes too simple sometimes too complicated.
Usually a pleasure.
Using up maths books, not wasting space.
Fractions are spectacular.
Angles are exciting.
Multiplication is excellent.
And addition is superb.
Subtraction is OK but not my favourite.
But the best is division.
It couldn't be better.
Maths is a world of luxury.
Don't you think so too?

Mischa Wykurz (9)
Coppermill Primary School

THE WIND IS AN EAGLE

Eagles fly fast in the sky
Like wind in the sky hunting
Never landing on the ground.
Sounds like wind when flapping its wings.

Adeel Ahmed (8)
Coppermill Primary School

SCHOOL POEM

Supply teacher speaks another language.
Gives us German work that we cannot read.
She smokes like hell,
and she is always speaking.
She smells like she has not had
a wash for a long time.
Art is the best subject but she does boring English.
She is always grumbling, and she is always ratty.
She is really fat.
Always breaking computers, and she is always chewing on the pencil.
She has ten cups of tea an hour.
She is a mess, big-time and she is really bossy.

James Murchison (9)
Coppermill Primary School

SCHOOL POEM

Teachers shouting and children talking.
Teachers who make us do hard English.
Some teachers who are very helpful.
Teachers who don't mark your work.
Lumpy teachers who swear when they're crazy.
All the teachers decide what's going to happen on trips.
Supply teachers who give us easy work.
Usual teachers give us hard work.

Tayub Ahmed (10)
Coppermill Primary School

SCHOOL DINNERS

School dinners are revolting don't you think?
There's lumpy custard that make you wanna commit suicide,
Mushy peas and cheese puffs just make you wanna puke.

But not all dinners are horrible
Because there are:
Miraculous cakes, cream and sweets
Ice-cream with strawberries
Apples, bananas, cherries,
Doesn't it make your mouth water.

Kala Patel (10)
Coppermill Primary School

PLAYTIME

Infants in the playground screaming
We don't have to work which is great
Playful children galloping around.
The best time is playtime.
Boys using bad language
Masterful teachers on playground duty
Boys playing football
Boys kicking the footballs in your face
Oh I wish we could ban boys from playing football!

Zoe Buckley (10)
Coppermill Primary School

LIFE AT SCHOOL

School is where you gain your knowledge,
It's supposed to be full of fun.
But sometimes, just sometimes, I get bored
When all my work is done.
And playtimes are so short, you know,
They don't give time for us.
The whole idea is to get some fresh air
Then back to school-time fuss.
While I work till dinner
Hunger builds up inside me.
And by working so hard on paper and card
I start to feel all dizzy.
Then out we go to dinner play,
And we think and think about the food,
My friends and I wait and wait,
But dinner is always late.
Then play is over
And teachers rule again.
Some children are naughty
But don't get the cane.
When home-time comes
I wait for my brother.
Then we both race home
To my waiting mother.

Tabassum Saboley (10)
Coppermill Primary School

SCHOOL LIFE

Bossy teachers shouting a lot.
Crooked line so teacher doesn't let us in.
Talking on carpet so teacher says, 'Face the wall.'
Talking in quiet reading,
End up in another teacher's classroom who is in.
Not opening books in quiet reading,
Read by Miss O'Brien's desk.
Not working fast, work, work in dinner-time.
Wriggle with a pencil, sit on the carpet.
Moving after the whistle, be yelled at very loudly.

Mohammed Fayyad (9)
Coppermill Primary School

SCHOOL POEM

In the changing room girls and boys are very noisy.
A cold shower before the pool.
Horrible pool but, encouraging teachers.
Hats don't go on properly.
People mostly get jammed lockers.
People lose clothes and 50ps.
It is very exciting at the pool.
But not when you drown.

Cassie White (9)
Coppermill Primary School

SCHOOL POEM

Boys playing football, a spectacular goal.
Freezing playground, oh it's like the North Pole.
Smelly toilets, oh what a foul stench.
Lumpy custard, foul and filthy, don't want to eat that.
Plump teachers on the run *aahhhhh! Help*.
Fun art, excellent, want to do more.
Fantastic swimmer, I'm awesome.
Scary teachers, really creepy.
Teachers grumbling, they don't like me.
Fascinating books, these are wicked, more quiet reading please.

Nathan Grindley (9)
Coppermill Primary School

SCHOOL POEM

Monstrous teachers, moan, moan, moan,
Extraordinary playtimes, yes playtime,
Excellent maths, that's easy,
Giggling girls laughing at jokes,
Boring English, I'm getting tired,
Smelly toilets, can you smell that?
Beastly school dinners *yuck!*
Endless work going on and on,
Easy spellings, I got that one right.

Chantel Brownbill (10)
Coppermill Primary School

SCHOOL

Sometimes dinner ladies can be helpful,
but usually they are dreadful.
That's why I'm a pack-lunch person.
I hate grumpy cooks,
they just copy from books.
Ask for more
you become a real bore.
Complain about food
the cook gets in a bad mood.
Once I ate a school dinner and it was filthy.
How could people eat that stuff?
Sometimes dinner ladies can be helpful,
but usually they are dreadful.
That's why I'm a pack-lunch person.

Beth Kelly (9)
Coppermill Primary School

SCHOOL POEM

Boring maths it's so hard for me.
Silly children in the playground.
Good teachers smiling.
Children screaming at spiders on the carpet.
Children crying in the playground because
no one is their friend.
Children don't listen to their teachers.
Children running at school supposed to be walking.
Teachers get cross with the children screeching their chairs.
Boys are playing football and that's not fair on the girls.
In the playground I never have time to play football
because of the boys.

Saira Mahmood (10)
Coppermill Primary School

SCHOOL LIFE

Easy maths fills me with joy,
Pleasant times tables test makes me cheerful,
Tedious science gets on my nerves,
Endless work is monotonous,
Hard fractions are awful,
Messy art is horrible,
Confusing history makes me sad,
But Ancient Greeks are great to learn about.

Billy Green (9)
Coppermill Primary School

COSMIC

I am a person from outer space
In a space shuttle shaped like a face
I landed on Mars with a lot of scars
Thinking whatever to do,
I am very bored with a dirty old sword
Sitting on a very flat board,
I am a person from outer space
Playing around on the solar system's face
My next stop was the sun
But I found it wasn't much fun,
I am a person from outer space
In a space shuttle shaped like a face,
If you see me even once
I suggest you should run like you've only done once.

Faiyaz Patel (10)
Davies Junior School

ALIENS

I sometimes dream of big blue aliens,
that live all the way on Mars.
They have hundreds and hundreds of eyes,
and a humungous mouth but no ears.
I wish they could come to Earth,
and steal all the teachers from school,
that would be more than cool.
I'd tell them to come to my house,
and we could party all night.
I could show them to my neighbours,
and give them a real fright.
But I wouldn't show them to everyone,
especially not my mum.
If everybody found out it wouldn't be much fun.
So one day if aliens do come to Earth,
I'll get to them first.

Tia Ingram (11)
Davies Junior School

ALIEN FROM MARS

I'm the alien from Mars,
I look like a blue elephant.
I always wear a fake skin,
So nobody finds out,
That I'm from Mars.
Now I'm in a clothes shop,
I'm looking at clothes to wear,
So I can look good,
Now I'm going to run out with a Mars Bar,
I'm going back to Mars, bye!

Asam Zaman (11)
Davies Junior School

ALIEN

I am an alien,
From outer space
I have two heads,
Three eyes, yellow hair, green teeth.
My best friend is made from beef
He has false teeth,
Horns on his chin.
My spaceship is made from a waste paper bin.
My friend comes from Mars,
I come from Uranus we are invading the Earth
For someone to train us to talk to walk to be polite.
Not to cause a massive fight.

Alisha McFarlane (11)
Davies Junior School

MARS

I am from Mars, over there we eat cars,
We like them so much, especially the clutch,
But, I eat stars as you can see,
Because I am just a baby.
I am from outer space,
I want to destroy the human race.
But before I could, we had to go to the boring place.
I have lots of stars,
If you touch them I will eat all your Mars Bars,
And take your cars.

Irfan Farooqui (10)
Davies Junior School

SPACE AT NIGHT

I was asleep
in my warm, snug bed,
not a squeak,
the sky was red.
Light had not gone,
the stars were out,
it was as bright as ever
when the lights were out.
I woke, aliens were flying,
in their flying saucers,
they whizzed by,
with their sons and daughters.
The planets
at four in the morning,
look brilliant
as they vanish.
But most of all
the moon's the best.
Is it cheese?
It's better than the rest.
With its blinding light,
a magnificent sight
it shines all night.
All the planets, stars,
aliens and the moon
they're all splendid
but night's gone too soon.
They're all vanishing
by five a.m.
so goodbye
to them!

Susannah Haynes (10)
Davies Junior School

PLANETS

First is Mercury which is very lurky.
Second is Venus which thinks it's a genius.
Third is Earth where women give birth.
Fourth is Mars which smokes cigars.
Fifth is Jupiter which gets stupider and stupider.
Sixth is Saturn which has a nice pattern.
Seventh is Uranus which is contagious.
Eighth is Neptune which sings a very nice tune.
Ninth is Pluto which loves playing Cluedo.

Kirsty Louise Green (11)
Davies Junior School

NARS FROM MARS

My name is Nars from the planet Mars,
My favourite food is superstars,
They're nice and squashy like Milky Bars,
You wouldn't know how they are,
I really like them, oh yes I do,
If you touch them I'll give you my flu,
Or maybe I could come after *you!*
I'll hunt you down using my claws,
And I'll eat you using my paws,
Or maybe I'll see you at dawn,
But anyhow I'm coming!

Rajiv Patel (11)
Davies Junior School

OUR NINE PLANETS

Our solar system is nice,
It has nine planets plus the sun,
Mercury and Venus hot and rocky,
No living things to play hockey,
Earth is wonderful 'cause it has life,
Human beings and also mice!
Mars is lonely, quiet and dry,
If you went there you'd be sure to cry,
Jupiter is large, largest of them all,
But saddest of all it doesn't have a mall!
Saturn is pretty,
But it's a pity,
That we don't live there,
And it's just not fair!
Uranus is small,
But of course bigger than a ball,
Neptune is freezy,
But not too squeezy,
Pluto is tiny and icy cold,
If you went there, oh do be bold!

Anna Rashid (10)
Davies Junior School

FEAR FROM DARK

Dark is a monster reaching to get you,
Dark is playing with my fear.
Dark is loud fighting noises,
Dark is twisting, whirlwind blistering.
Dark is your eyes watering and wet,
Scary and dark on a blustery day.

Dark is your room twisting on a spot,
Dark is things moving to different places.
Dark, I'm scared, if ghosts are real.
Dark is eyes watching you around.
Dark is hands playing with my fear.
Scary and dark on a blustery day.

Haniyyah Rashid (7)
Forest Prep School

THE DARK NIGHT

Dark creeps around me
I dive under the covers
It's dark under there

It touches me
I'm cold!
I shiver

The wind howls outside
Something bashes against the window
I jump up!
I run to the window
The wind still howls

Dark is deathly evil
Vampires appear in my head
Hands play with my fear

Starlight fills the room
The sun rises
The wind dies down

It is morning
I never forget the dreaded night.

Francesca Fox (8)
Forest Prep School

AUTUMN

It was an autumn day,
everything swayed,
Autumn never goes my way,
overall it is okay.

All leaves change colour,
Some with the other,
Autumn is fun,
all things are over and done.

All my friends love conkers,
a lot of them go bonkers,
everything is everywhere,
then the sun comes out next year.

Conkers fall off the trees,
they fall onto my knee,
sometimes it rains,
onto the plains.

Devpal Bhachu (10)
Forest Prep School

HARVEST POEM

Harvest time is here once more,
Acorns and conkers are swept away,
Rake up those leaves and collect the hay,
Voice your joy this autumn day,
Edible foods are again collected,
Stored away in jars for winter,
Thank you, Lord, for these gifts of life.

Nicholas Bertenshaw (9)
Forest Prep School

WINTER POEM

The chill in the winter breeze
Could make a snowman freeze.

The ice on the pond
Is good for skating on.

The snow that is falling down
Does cover the leaves that are brown.

The people are slipping on the ice
Which isn't really very nice.

Although the people are very cold
They are also very bold.

The people get a ball of snow
And what they do is throw.

Jamie Bajer (9)
Forest Prep School

AUTUMN

Autumn is a time when you play conkers.
Smash them, hit them, squash them, swish them.
Down they go to the ground in pieces,
You cry out in anger while you see your opponent cheering.
Multi-coloured leaves fall off the trees,
Booming and zooming, fireworks go,
Crunching leaves make squirrels alert,
They run away scattering the dirt.
Then they climb up trees for their food
And munch them and crunch them in a mood.

Bryn Williams (9)
Forest Prep School

SEASONS

Spring spring it gets warm
Spring spring birds in form
Spring spring red as roses
Spring spring here comes posies.

Summer summer the sun comes out
Summer summer plants fully sprout
Summer summer bees collect pollen
Summer summer have a lolly.

Autumn autumn the leaves are brown
Autumn autumn makes me frown
Autumn autumn it gets cold
Stay inside be very bold.

Winter winter the sun goes down
Winter winter autumn has drowned
Winter winter summer's dead
Winter winter the season we dread

Chris Facey (9)
Forest Prep School

FRIENDS

Once I had a friend but he really drove me round the bend
He chased me round and round until he fell upon the ground.
He took me to see Rolf Harris but I felt a bit embarrassed.

Once I had a friend, I think he was quite dumb
Because he stuck needles in his thumb
Other boys started to laugh and I felt very daft
My friends always asked me to play even if it was a rainy day.

Friends! What a fuss!

Alex Denham (9)
Forest Prep School

THE FOOTBALL MATCH

The crowd were singing loud
and proud.
The crowd were chanting loud
and proud.
The players too were shouting but
at something else. I wonder who.
The ref, of course, who else.
He kept on blowing his whistle.
It looked like he wouldn't be stopping.
But that's a football match for you.
And when the final whistle was blown,
The stadium was only half full.

Jack Keating (9)
Forest Prep School

GRENDEL

A Fen lurker
  A rancid stinker
    A night killer
      A blood trailer
        A land destroyer
          A creature horrifier
            A living creature crusher
              A monster muncher
                A flesh ripper
                  An eyeball eater
                    A scream maker
                      A land slitherer.

William Penney (8)
Forest Prep School

THE ORCHESTRA

The trumpet is loud and so is the horn
They never allow the audience to yawn.

The violin squeaks and the bass plays low
The cello whines as the melody flows.

The flute sings high and the clarinet mellows
The trombone moves about while the tuba just bellows.

The drums are fierce in the middle of the stage
They sound like a lion inside its cage.

The cymbals clash, the quiet they shatter
The triangles tingle and the percussion just clatter.

The guitars strum the tune, while the harpist plucks
The bagpipes hum and the accordion sucks.

Now let's go into an easier thing
How about the conductor - what about him?

He taps his baton on his musical stand
And waves it along with the band.

Without him we will have earplugs in our ears
But with him, the music will make us shed tears.

You have to hum it, strum it, pluck it and blow it
This is the orchestra - as we know it!

Alex Levy (9)
Forest Prep School

FOOTBALL

'I want the ball, I want the ball,'
I'm looking for support.
'I've got the ball, I've got the ball,'
Oh no, I might be caught.

I look and see the keeper,
Spread his arms out wide.
I keep my cool and slip the ball
Right past his side.

'I've scored, I've scored,'
I run past the half-way line.
My team-mates shout 'Oh what a goal,
Right in extra time.'

Matthew Fowler (10)
Forest Prep School

AUTUMN

In autumn when the leaves start to fall,
And people sweep them up in piles so tall,
In America they call it the Fall,
It is definitely the best season of all.

Shops start selling guys,
To put on a bonfire on a pole that is so tall,
It is definitely the best season of all.

Conkers start falling from the horse chestnut trees,
And children make holes to put string through,
They bake them, vinegar them, varnish them and all,
It is definitely the best season of all.

George Murphy (9)
Forest Prep School

WHAT SHOULD I BE?

'Should I be a nun?'
'Na, there's no point.'
'Should I fly a plane?'
'Na, that's boring.'
'Should I be a cook?'
'Na, I hate peeling onions.'
'Or should I be a teacher.'
'Mmm, yeah that's it.
I'll be a teacher and be really kind,
But when they're naughty they'll
Get chills down their spines.
Into detention, move, move, move,
Extra prep for you young man.'

Emma Oliver (9)
Forest Prep School

BAD BOYS

Mrs Spice! Mrs Spice!
Luke here is not being nice
He stole my pencil and took my rubber
And then he called me a load of blubber.

Mrs Spice! Mrs Spice!
Tim here is not being nice
He stamped on my foot, said I was fat
Then he said I look ugly in my hat.

Mrs Spice! Mrs Spice!
Craig here is not being nice
He punched my back, bumped into me
And then he kicked me on the knee.

Oh, James my lad you poor, poor dear
You really must be feeling queer
These bullies must be made to stop
Or I won't allow them in my shop.

James Dobias (9)
Forest Prep School

WHAT IS BLUE?

Up in the bright blue sky,
The blue tits fly by,
Chasing kingfishers,
Hear them cry!

Down below the waters,
The blue whale swims by,
Watching fish who lie,
On the seabed looking at the sky.

In the meadow bluebells grow tall,
Making a carpet for us all.
Children play happily,
Blue eyes sparkling like sapphires.

Blue is the best of them all!

Lucy Boggis (9)
Forest Prep School

SPRING

Flowers are yellow
Blueberries are blue,
Where is the sun?
Give us a clue.
Look left, look right,
There it is! No, that's a kite.
There's the sun
It's over there.
Let's go to the fair.

The bees hum
As the children come
With their mum,
But the child was stung
On his thumb.

Pranav Bhanot (9)
Forest Prep School

A CAT

A night singer,
A four footer,
A fireside sitter,
A ball player,
A wild jumper,
A mat sitter,
A wet licker,
A wild runner,
A fence walker,
A bed sleeper.

Aneet Baxi (8)
Forest Prep School

MUSHY PEAS!

I hate mushy peas!
Too mushy for my taste
But my grandad loves them
Has them with his potatoes
Has them with his chips
But I hate them!

I hate mushy peas!
Too mushy for my taste
I hate the sauce they come in
I hate their mushy insides
I don't believe people eat them!
And I hate them!

Thomas Whittle (10)
Forest Prep School

AUTUMN

When the leaves turn red,
And you snuggle up in your cosy bed,
Do you know what's happening,
In the dawning of the morning?
Do you listen to the fireworks,
Blow up in the sky,
Then come down like silver birch scattered like a pie?
Can you hear the autumn's leaves,
Swinging in the breeze?
Can you hear them?
Because I definitely can.

Michael Burgoyne (9)
Forest Prep School

AUTUMN

The weather is getting cold,
I find it very dull,
Leaves falling down,
Yellow, green, brown.

The days are getting shorter,
The nights are getting darker,
Autumn is here,
Winter is near.

Conkers are falling,
Children collect conkers,
Sometimes an exchange,
This gives them a change.

Sukhjit Bains (10)
Forest Prep School

THE HERON

T he heron swoops and dives for fish.
H eron loves her golden dish
E legant legs has she.

H eron dives back to its den
E very feather on her face always grows in beauty and grace.
R acing through the sky above
O ver rushing water streams and Wanstead Park
N othing beats the heron.

Georgina Lily Webb (7)
Forest Prep School

WINTER

Winter is cold with lots of snow,
Winter is when children's noses glow,
Winter is rain and fog,
Winter is snow upon a log,
Winter is rain upon a window-sill,
Winter is when children get a chill,
Winter is all things wet,
Winter is bad for some pets,
Winter is a blanket of snow,
Winter is when rivers don't flow,
Winter is lots of storms,
Winter is cold, you need to keep warm,
Winter is when you have to wear a thick vest,
Winter is the best!

Charlotte Harris (11)
Forest Prep School

HORSE

Clip-clopper,
Mud-squelcher,
Hay-muncher,
Messy-food scooper,
Show-jumper,
Fur-moulter,
Good-galloper,
Wild-canterer,
Slow-trotter,
Good-friend,
Tired-pony.

Katie Pickering (8)
Forest Prep School

KENNING CAT

Whisker-twitcher
Tail- wagger
Milk-lapper
Stroke-lover
Fence-climber
Long-sleeper
Sofa-scratcher
Washing-tail
Catty-stamper
Fish-eater
Tiger-family
Fierce-fighter
Warm-sleeper
Carpet-lounger

Victoria Rose Havercroft (8)
Forest Prep School

SHADOWS

Shadows are like ghosts creeping behind me.
Shadows are like another of you.
Shadows follow you everywhere.

Shadows appear only in the dark.
Shadows are stuck to your feet.
Shadows follow you everywhere.

Shadows have to be with you.
But shadows do not speak or eat.
But shadows follow you everywhere.

Amie Kingsnorth (8)
Forest Prep School

A NIGHTMARE SPELL

Hubble, bubble, boil and trouble,
Mix it up and make it rumble.

In the cauldron go,
All the nasty things we throw,
Leg of lizard, eye of dog,
Tongue of bat and toe of frog.

Hubble, bubble, boil and trouble,
Mix it up and make it rumble.

What a horrible potion we'll make,
When all these things are boiled and baked,
Newt's eye and owl's wing,
When you mix it, it might go *'Ping!'*

Hubble, bubble, boil and trouble,
Mix it up and make it rumble.

Mix it all together now,
You'll find you'll have a horrible spell,
When you see the cauldron bubble,
You'll be sure it will make some trouble.

Hubble, bubble, boil and trouble,
Mix it up and make it rumble.

Laura Murray (9)
Forest Prep School

BOIL AND BUBBLE

Round and round, round we go,
Casting spells as we throw.

Make this come a wicked spell,
Round we go, steaming hot.
Bubbling black, a dirty pot.
Double, double toil and trouble.
Make this one a girl that bubbles.

Round and round, round we go;
Casting spells as we throw.

Let this in the cauldron boil,
Lizards, frogs and a touch of oil.

Bring the bats and bake the cats,
Skin the snake and put in the rats.

Round and round, round we go,
Casting spells as we throw.

Is it boiling? Let me see.
Make this one a wicked spell.
Cool it down with a bat's blood.
Do I see something wicked?
Boil it and bake it and make it wicked.

Nisa Sekhon (9)
Forest Prep School

Autumn Is...

Autumn is September, October and November,
Autumn is coming back to school,
Autumn is whooshing winds.
Autumn is Open Day and you can see our lovely displays.

Autumn is a time for harvest,
Autumn is farmers cutting the crops.
Autumn is wheat, rye and barley,
Autumn is harvest which gives us food.

Autumn is spooky, scary Hallowe'en,
Autumn is pumpkins with sparkling candles
Inside them and evil spirits.
Autumn is fretful trick or treaters,
Autumn is lingering witches and vampires
Waiting at your door.

Autumn is Guy Fawkes Night,
Autumn is exploding gunpowder and
Bewildered fireworks!

Autumn is crunching leaves and cracking twigs,
Autumn is spiky shells with shiny conkers inside.
Autumn is acorns dropping from enormous oak trees.
Autumn is half-term.

Autumn is crackling, whishing, spluttering
Bonfires with tasty marshmallows.
Autumn is misty fog and damp swamps.
Autumn is rainbows with their fading colours:
Red, yellow, green, blue, orange, violet and indigo.

Cristina Cooney (8)
Forest Prep School

CITY LIFE

Litter and dirt, everywhere you go,
Tall scruffy buildings, never very low.
Petrol fumes from the cars, miles away down the road,
Trucks always halting to deliver their heavy load.
Businessmen talking away, on their mobile phones,
All the tramps in cardboard boxes, haven't any homes.
Walking through the park with the wildlife all around,
No-one would believe that down the street is town.
The hustle, the bustle, the excitement of the lights,
You never would have guessed that the lights are so bright.
People coming out of Harvey Nicholls,
Have so many bags that it tickles.
The Tower of London and Big Ben,
Seem to beckon all of the children.
I love going to London, to shop and see all the sights,
But I hate to see all the tramps and homeless, because they give me a fright!

Laura Thorogood (11)
Forest Prep School

LIONS

Lions shine in the dark like stars.
Lions are as bright as the golden sun.
Lions sleep in the wild wind.
Lions growl like a hurricane.
Lions chase their food as quickly as lightning.
Lions fight like a million soldiers.
Lions' teeth are as sharp as a sword.
Lions' tails swish like tree branches.
Lions' legs are like an automatic machine.

Charlotte Elise Hall (8)
Forest Prep School

A BOOK

Hard words,
Easy words,
Short words,
Long words,
Strange words,
Familiar words,
That's a book!

                    Words,
                    Time,
                    Space,
                    Imagination,
                    Trouble,
                    Colours,
                    That's a book!

Hidden treasure,
Romance,
Mystery,
Adventure,
Cunning plans,
Narrow escapes,
That's a book!

                    Next stop,
                    Page two
                    What's in here?
                    I must find out.
                    More imagination,
                    More adventures,
                    More words.

That's a book!

Megan Greet (8)
Forest Prep School

SHADOWS

Shadows creep behind me,
Shadows touch my face,
Shadows follow me everywhere.
Shadows are scary,
Shadows are different spirits.
Shadows catch all my fear,
Shadows are like waterfalls dripping.
Shadows shout at me.
Shadows are inside me.
Shadows are like cushions with teeth.
Shadows appear everywhere.
Shadows eat with you,
Shadows copy you.
Shadows do things with you.
Shadows bring other shadows.

Janel Korhaliller (8)
Forest Prep School

DARK

Dark is when hands play with my fear,
Ghostly sounds are what I hear,
Hands are creeping up my spine,
Ghosts and spirits wail and whine.

Softly tread the feet of the dead,
Filling my heart with fear and dread,
Dark is where nothing can escape,
Covering everything with its long black cape.

Wolves howling on the hills,
Giving my warm body chills,
Eyes staring out at me,
In my mind for me to see.

Frankensteins and monsters in my head,
Fear and doom are in my bed,
As I wish for the sun so heavenly,
In my head dark is deathly!

Georgina Leighton (7)
Forest Prep School

DARK

Dark is hands touching
My feet and spine.
Dark is like falling
Into a hole in the ground.

Dark is people creeping
Behind me and looking at me
Dark is like hands
Like vampires and ghosts.

Dark is like people shutting
The door and creeping under
My bed at night
Dark is ghosts looking at me.

Dark is ghosts in
My bed at night.
Dark is ghosts watching
Me at my door.

Sarah Campbell (7)
Forest Prep School

TERRORS

Terrors are like the dark death
Terrors are like falling off a mountain
Terrors are like a life burning
Terrors are like a wolf howling
Terrors are like hands playing with your fears
Terrors are like heavy hail falling
Terrors are like a haunted house
Terrors are like human bones
Terrors are like flooding waters going over me
Terrors are like ghosts touching me
Terrors are like vampires biting me
Terrors are like a bed with wide jaws
Terrors are like scares and dares.

Abigail Evans (8)
Forest Prep School

KENNING'S MOUTH

Biscuit   -   Cruncher
Teeth   -   Sparkler
Milk   -   Drinker
Three   -   Gapper
Talk   -   Talker
Height   -   Shouter
Bradley   -   Screamer
Ryan   -   Kisser
Clown   -   Laughter
Food   -   Gobbler

Melissa Kaye (8)
Forest Prep School

CAT

Mouse-catcher
Milk-drinker
Whisker-twitcher
Pillow-scratcher
Settee-sitter
Fence-climber
Mat-lounger
Street-walker
Bird-chaser
Biscuit-eater
Pussy-footer
Bushy-tailer
Lion family
Pat-lover
Fierce fighter
Tail-wagger
Fish-eater
Long-napper
Night-player
Tree-sitter
Fast runner
Bright-eyer
Sharp-clawer
Long-teether.

Lucy Pottinger (8)
Forest Prep School

The Barn

The barn is a great big umbrella,
Sheltering people from the weather.

The creaking of the barn is the crying of the ghosts,
The light coming through is like dim lampposts.

The strong beams on the roof are tree trunks being cut down,

The hay on the floor is your warm bed at home,
The shadows which in the night begin to roam.

The stones of the barn bring memories of home farms,
The barn seems different to other barns.

The noises outside are the animals weeping,
Inside you can hear people weeping.

The barn is a great big umbrella,
Sheltering people from the weather.

Sophie Munday (10)
Forest Prep School

Night

The tranquillity and stillness of the air,
The hoots and scrambles are all you can hear.

The moon is a torch, glowing out,
To calm you down in times of doubt.

The fluffy clouds hiding the moon,
But they move away very soon.

The stars are the sparkles in cats' eyes,
Twinkling like jewels in disguise.

The owls' and badgers' eyes are peeping,
While the other animals are quietly sleeping.

The wind calling to the nation of the night,
Until darkness changes to light.

Priya Malhotra (11)
Forest Prep School

THE BARN

Creepy shadows in the night,
You open your eyes and they're in your sight.

Creaks in the wooden beams,
Through the cracks in the door the sun does gleam.

The gaps in the wall are eyes peeping out at you,
The howls at night are the ghosts waiting to say *'Boo!'*

A gust of wind on a winter's day,
And I hope that soon they will go away.

The roof of the barn is as high as the sky,
If there was a hole in it you would see birds go by.

If you tread on the floor it will sound like a mouse,
As if it were under there making its house.

Stephanie Neary (11)
Forest Prep School

Fear

When the candlelight flickers,
The demons dance about.
When the light goes out,
The darkness haunts our fears.

When hunger strikes,
All joy is lost.
When the food runs out,
The children are left to starve.

When the plague comes near,
Families fear for their lives.
When people lie dying,
All hope is lost.

Melanie Stevens (11)
Forest Prep School

The Dark

Dark creeps behind me.
Dark brown hands touch my hand.
Dark is deathly to me.
Dark is vampires.
Dark is hands playing with my fears.
Dark touching my cheeks.
Dark is the sunset going away.
Dark is like a computer screen.
Dark is when a ghost appears.
Dark is terrifying and black.
Dark is the hidden sun.

Elizabeth Pope (8)
Forest Prep School

MY SHADOW

My shadow creeps behind me.
    She hardly ever goes,
    My shadow's always with me.

    She makes her way back home when she's sad,
    She can be happy,
    She can be bad.
    My shadow's always with me.

    My shadow walks with me,
    She talks with me.
    My shadow's always with me.

    When I look behind,
    My shadow looks behind with me.
    My shadow's always with me.

    She eats with me,
    She sleeps with me.
    She is my best friend.
    My shadow's always with me.

    But when the sun goes in,
    She makes a din as she follows
    Me round the bend.
    My shadow's always with me.

Hannah Whittle (7)
Forest Prep School

The Barn

The moon is a big white plate,
Look at the birds, watch them mate.
The door creaks, along the floor,
Look out the barn, across the moors.

The windows are slowly shut,
We lie down in our little hut,
The shutters are pulled down,
And we wear a frown.

We all are forlorn,
On this bright early morn.
The splashes of the puddle,
The joy of Mother's bundle.

The darkness of the barn,
The noises of Maggie Hogg's farm.
The sounds of the two children asleep,
While Catherine sits in the straw and weeps.

Siobhan McElroy (10)
Forest Prep School

The Hidden Barn

The creak of the wooden door,
Is the cry of the black swallow.

The gleam through the solid rocks,
Is the eye of the sun.

The rustle in the meadow hay,
Is the bustle of the mouse.

The gaps in the roof,
Are the gleaming stars.

The gaps in the roof,
Are like silver bars.

The pitch-blackness inside the barn,
Is like the night outside, in the cold.

Stephanie Moi (11)
Forest Prep School

UNCERTAINTIES

With a bang on the door,
With a creak of the floor.
With a squeak in the hay,
And the happiness of the day.

With the howl of a wolf,
With the rustling of the bush.
With the splashes of the river,
And with the squeak of the mouse.

With the life of the plants,
With the death of the six children.
With the misery of Maggie Hoggs,
And the joy of one and the hate of the other.

With the chill in her finger,
With the coldness in her eye.
With the ice on the frosty grass,
And the dark blue sky.

Aiyna Singh (11)
Forest Prep School

FEELINGS OF CATHERINE

The hope of Mum coming home,
And the sound of Dan's tired moan.
The hatred in Maggie Hogg's eye,
As she approached to tell us why,
We should not be protected from the plague,
Which swept through the village in a couple of days.
The fear of the plague coming to the barn,
The thought of not having Mum's caring arms,
To calm you down when you are stressed,
And relax when you are feeling tense.
The fear in my mother's heart,
When she had to let us go,
It must have been hard,
For her and for me,
Because I was given a huge responsibility,
To look after Dan and Tessa,
And to make this time a whole lot better.
The excitement of berry-picking,
Especially for Dan,
Whose lips he likes licking.
The boredom of picking sticks all day,
To keep a fire in the barn of hay.
The thankfulness of Dick Mossop for his juicy rabbit,
We broiled in a stew, which warmed up Clem
               when he staggered through,
To us while infected with the plague,
I knew I had a hard decision to make.
Should I leave him and let him die
Or should I bring him in and risk three young children's lives?
What on earth would my mother do?
I need to think about the other two!

Lauren Sewell (11)
Forest Prep School

THE OLD CRUCK BARN

The barn was a shelter for many people,
It kept them safe and out of danger,
The children's laughs and happy cries
Were like the bells of a church steeple.

The old barn's beams creaked like old bones,
The wind howled round and was bitterly cold,
But when the children played and had great fun,
It seemed the cosiest of all homes.

The barn's safe feeling was like being at home,
It had a roof and strong walls too,
It gave a feeling of safe security,
But the barn was left to moan.

Rosie Boggis (11)
Forest Prep School

HOPE

The hope of survival,
Against the plague.
The hope of comfort,
From our mother.
The hope for food,
Against starvation.
The hope for warmth,
From the cold.
The hope for Clem,
Against illness.
The hope for health,
From death.

Hemali Patel (11)
Forest Prep School

CHILDREN OF WINTER

The joy of dancing and playing games,
The sound of birds on a spring or summer's day,
The protection of the warm and cosy hay,
Catherine's imagination on a good day.

The fear of Maggie Hogg's hating eyes,
The look on Mother's face when she leaves us,
                                I want to cry,
The fear of being left alone,
Dan's annoying moans and groans.

The blackberry patches on the moors,
The old oak wood used for the barn door,
The trickling stream with clean, pure water,
Tessa's smile and her laughter.

Sophia Vanezis (10)
Forest Prep School

SCHOOL DINNERS

Some school dinners are really nice,
Like chicken tikka and rice.
Some are good, some are not,
Some are cold, some are hot.
When they're yucky, and some are,
You can always use the salad bar.
Hotplate 1 and hotplate 2,
The choice is always up to you.

Monday is a surprise,
Tuesday, hot food arrives,
Wednesday is never the same,
Thursday, *oh no!* Not hot-pot again!
Friday is the best of all when bangers
                    and chips are at our lips!
But thank goodness, when the weekend comes,
We all eat at our mum's
          and have fat tums!

Philippa Mansbridge (9)
Forest Prep School

THE BARN

The barn is dull,
It's very dark.
The barn is spooky,
Not even one spark.

Noises are heard,
The creaky door.
Holes in the walls,
The stone-cold floor.

The sun comes in,
A little light,
But very hot,
And awfully bright.

The wind comes in,
The sun goes out,
The barn is hidden,
No one about.

Kirnjit Nijjer (11)
Forest Prep School

CITY LIFE

The city is a busy place
Old friends coming face to face
Cars zooming off to their destination
Or catch the tube from the station.
Businessmen are not funny
Being serious making money.
Mothers shouting,
Children scream,
Palaces, churches, museums all gleam.

The country on the other hand
It has a lot of greener land,
Where children have fun
And farmers make hay
Growing food for our tables day by day.
The country is a quiet place,
The village show
The point-to-point race.
Fathers, sons, daughters, mothers
People make time to talk to each other.

A busy town or a country life?
Buses or horses?
I know which is my choice!

Katie Hulin (11)
Forest Prep School

The Moon

It's a gigantic silver cricket ball
It's a dusty white-washed wall.

It's a cracked dish,
It's an eye of a fish,
It's a melon or a lemon.

It's a scoop of vanilla ice-cream,
It's a light-bulb with a silver beam.

It's a fluff of cotton wool,
It's a night sun shining on our lawn.

Poppy Bristow (11)
Forest Prep School

The Knight And His Lady

The brave knight fought a battle,
On his very own,
Only his king could help him,
As all his knights had gone.

The knight's lovely lady
Sitting alone,
She was very worried,
Waiting for him to come.

At last, a few days later,
He returned home,
What happened to his king?
Nobody knows.

Katie Turner (9)
Gatehouse School

THE LOST NIGHT

In the fields stood a knight,
Tall in stature, strong in structure,
With black-blue bruised-like armour,
He had a dark brown steed,
With a pointed red saddle,
His sword like a rose thorn,
The shield with a proud lion roaring away.
One tree casts a shadow upon the huge giant.
Where does he come from?
What is he doing?
Nobody shall ever know why he stands there
                                    day and night.

James Paul Dale (10)
Gatehouse School

KNIGHT AT ARMS

In dark-towered Camelot,
Stands the knight at arms.
His armour gold and bright
Next to his pacing steed,
With sword and scabbard on his hip,
A coat-of-arms is his pride,
Luck on either side.
Shield is polished like the sun
As he looks at the past
He knows
He's a *knight at arms!*

Jason Marsham (10)
Gatehouse School

THE RED KNIGHT'S LADY

She walks gracefully up the flight of stairs,
Her long soft silk gown dragging along,
Hurrying to see the handsome knight.
Knocks on the door,
Her scarlet cloak on the chair,
Her red roses
Pricked by the thorn of the stem.
Her passionate lips kiss
The soft lips of the knight.
She walks gracefully away
Shutting the door silently.

Sheillee Shah (11)
Gatehouse School

THE KNIGHT'S LADY

As she walks in her room,
The light is shining on her golden brown hair,
As she walks in her garden,
The sun is shining on her silk clothes
And the sunlight is shining in her hazelnut eyes,
Waiting for her knight in armour to come.
Look in her eyes and see
The love between them.

Gioksel Erzindjan (9)
Gatehouse School

THE SILVER KNIGHT

The knight's armour is heavy,
It is made of metal,
Silver as silver.

It is very hard the armour,
It walks very slowly,
It makes a loud noise
      when it walks.

He stands still,
Sword silver, shield silver,
Everything he wears is silver.

Mariam Nazir Banoo (10)
Gatehouse School

THE KNIGHT

I am a knight of Camelot,
I fight with all my might
And have vowed to serve King Arthur.
      If I do not do so,
      That will not be right
      For I have taken my oath.
When I come home battered and bruised
My lady is there to comfort me,
And here is my son, *my pride and my joy.*

Jay Donaldson (9)
Gatehouse School

THE SOUNDS OF THE SEA

Seagulls squawk
Over the quiet, gentle, rippling waves,
While the stones rattle
And move on the sand below.
A sudden wind blows up,
Whoosh! Swish!
A boat in the sea
Creaks and flaps,
While the seagulls
Hurriedly return to their nests.

Emily King (8)
Gatehouse School

SEASHORE SHIMMER SAND

Seashore, shimmering sand,
Shining very, very brightly,
Look once, look again,
Shimmering seashore.

Listen to the wailing waves,
Slithering slowly up the shore,
Sliding softly down again
Whish whosh waves!

Nisha Kumari Mehta (8)
Gatehouse School

ARIEL SPIRIT OF THE SEA

I am Ariel, spirit of the sea,
I love the sand, I love the sea,
I walk along long beaches here and there,
And stare at the sea from land.

I dive to the bottom of the sea to see,
My friends, coral, fish, whale and shark,
I fly above the sea and sand,
And wave to my friends from above.

Then I fly away for good,
And fly and fly away,
'I've gone to see the world' I told my friends
But never ever came back.

Roberta Makoni (8)
Gatehouse School

THE BEACH

I see sand and waters
A bay and seaweed.
I hear the splash against the rocks,
The waves high to the sky,
The birds sing their songs,
Children play in the waters,
They are laughing.

Zain Butt (8)
Gatehouse School

The Starting Of The Tempest

Come, come you Tempest
Come and take the test.
Make it hail, make it rain
But for heaven's sake do not strain.
Make the sea at its roughest,
Ask the wind to be its toughest!
Push, spray upon the sand.
There is a flood on the land,
Help! Help!
The people are shouting
Help! Help!

Jennet Lewis (9)
Gatehouse School

The Beach

Look at the sand on the beach,
It looks like small grains of sugar.
The awful crabs,
Might just give you a nab.
The thundering waves,
Fill up the small caves,
When the sun goes down on the sea,
The view is the best you will see.

Rowan Carreira (9)
Gatehouse School

BELOW THE SEA

Below the sea where fathers lie,
There are sounds that never die,
Sea nymphs sing
Ding, dong, ding!
Coral made from bones
Now look like stones.
Eyes that were once bright
Are now pearls of white
To see things alive
One must dive
Full fathoms five.

Zara Taraporvala (8)
Gatehouse School

THE SEA

The sands are yellow,
The waves are blue,
The sun is shining,
The birds are flying,
I hear sounds of splashing,
I'm swimming around,
I'm diving to the bottom,
Playing with the fish.

Hina Nazir (8)
Gatehouse School

My Lady

I seek through the forest,
And peek through the branches,
Sadly, there is no sight,
But I'll keep on looking till I find her!

Oh my dear lady, come back please,
I'll die for you,
High above the mountains,
Just let me glance at you.

Just let me know you are safe,
Marry me, I beg you,
My lady, we shall be married,
And live in a palace of life.

Jujhar Singh (9)
Gatehouse School

The Beach

Once my feet touched
The hot yellow sands
They were not burnt
Because of the waves
The coolest waves cooled
And the seagulls played
Their happy tunes
For this is a real beach.

Oliver Ingram (8)
Gatehouse School

THE KNIGHT AND HIS BRIDE

There was once a knight,
Who was waiting for his bride,
She did not come,
So he started to hum,
Something in the night is shining,
It was his bride's dress
Gleaming in the moonlight.

He ran to his lady,
Then took her hand,
Then they ran through the land.

Marvin McLean (9)
Gatehouse School

THE KNIGHT AND HIS LADY

The knight is riding his horse,
His lady is waiting for him,
She sees him on his horse
And runs to kiss him.
She is wearing a long, silky white dress,
'Where have you been?' she says.
'I have been hunting in the forest.'
The lady replies, 'I have missed you.'

Gulsun Shevket (9)
Gatehouse School

THE LADY OF THE NIGHT

The lady waits beneath the stars alone,
The lonely, long cold night goes on,
The bright moon shines down on her,
Lighting up the earth so dark,
Her heart beats strongly,
For a long time she has waited,
At last they meet,
His armour reflects her beauty,
The lady and her knight.

Nanci Lynch (9)
Gatehouse School

THE CHURCH

Church
Holy Bible
Stain glass windows
Funeral in church gardens
In church you get christened
Jesus looks down from the sky
Christmas is a special day
People believe in God
Jesus has disciples
I love
Jesus

Lisa Swaby (9)
Globe Primary School

PARK

Ducks are in the pond.
Cans are going into the bins.
Park keeper is looking for bad kids.
Flowers grow in the sun and have fun.
Birds fly out of the nest.
Kids go on the slide and come down.
Kids go on the swings and fly in the sky.
Mums sunbathe and have fun in the sun.

Cheryl Day (8)
Globe Primary School

MY BODY

On my chest is a wooden desk
On my nail there's a slimy snail
On my thumb there's a big round drum
On my leg there's an egg
On my back there's a sack
Great rhyming Lisa!

Lisa Merry (9)
Globe Primary School

BIRDS

Birds, birds they are so squeaky.
When you are so sleep, sleep, sleepy.
Squeaky, squeaky, squeaky birds.
Such a fuss when you are asleep.

Maice Browne (9)
Globe Primary School

MY HANDS

My hands
can
write and fight
can
lead and bleed
can
touch and feel
can
fly a kite
can
wobble and grab
can
hold things tightly
can
rub out things
can
catch a ball.

Amran Hussain (8)
Globe Primary School

MY HAND

My hands can write and rub out.
Can stretch and catch.
Can bleed and lead.
Can touch and feel.
They can even catch a ball.

My legs can walk and kick.
Can wear shoes and boots.
Can wear socks and tights.
They can even drive a car.

Fatima Begum (9)
Globe Primary School

My Hands Can

My hands can open a book.
My hands can move a baby.
My hands can put on a coat.
My hands can do a magic trick.
My hands can eat.
My hands can pick up a skipping rope.
My hands can do a lot of things now.

Shahnaz Alim (8)
Globe Primary School

My Hand

Can touch and feel
Can read and write
Can hold and drop
Can eat and drink
Can sleep and jump
Can see and hear
Can even climb and sharpen a pencil.

Shujana Begum (9)
Globe Primary School

The Train

Every morning at the break of day
I can hear so far away
The sound like voices in a dream!
The train in the station whistles and screams.

Jabir Hussain (8)
Globe Primary School

BLUE

Blue is the day time sky with the sun shining.
Blue is my Arsenal coat nice and warm inside.
Blue is the water at the seaside with the swirling waves, sssssshhhh.
Blue is the wallpaper with yellow flowers on it.
Blue is the furniture like a settee puffed up.

Barry Hanmore (9)
Globe Primary School

BLACK

Black is the horrible dull sky that makes the stars shine.
Black is the colour that people regret the most.
Black is the exciting colour of hair.
Black is the colour of a dull suit you wear for a funeral.
Black is also for the summer for exciting cool sunglasses.

Ryan Francois (9)
Globe Primary School

RED

Red - the blood inside our body.
Red - the red border in our class.
Red - the red jumper I am wearing.
Red - the colour of the sky when the sun sets.
Red - the red hand on the clock.

Stacey Rolfe (7)
Globe Primary School

SCHOOL SOUNDS

I can hear the people writing in their books.
I can hear the school diners eating their lunch.
I can hear people running and playing on the playground.
I can hear the bell ringing for people to line up.
I can hear the steel bands playing their chords.
I can hear the people warming up for PE time.

Eric Duong (8)
Globe Primary School

MY DOG

When I was small I dreamed of my dog.
My dog called me up to the sky, and he had wings so he could fly.
He showed me the stars, he showed me the moon and
he showed me the planets and then suddenly
when I woke up it was all gone.
I'll always remember.

Gizem Uluozen (9)
Globe Primary School

THE CAT

The cat went over the moon,
On a super sonic boom.
The cat took some porridge and a tent,
But when he landed the spoon got bent.
The cat said he didn't care,
And for all I know he's still up there.

Shofada Khanom (8)
Globe Primary School

MY MUM LIKES

My mum likes doing some sewing
And I can join her too.
My mum likes doing cooking
And I like eating rice.
My mum likes doing work
And I like doing some too.
I like doing anything.

Huma Yun (7)
Globe Primary School

LONDON UNDERGROUND

Underground, underground
deep and damp
Underground, underground
solid and smooth
Underground, underground
no light
dark as night.

Underground, underground
walls surround you like
the night
Underground, underground
trains go past
very very fast.

Underground, underground
stuck under the ground
while the starlit sky
goes flying by.

Amardip Marway (8)
Grangewood Independent School

A LOOK AT MODERN EGYPT

Mummies nest there
Over a thousand years
Day after day
Egypt has changed
Ropes on donkeys so they can't run
No cars but camels in the sun.

Egypt, Egypt
Gets different every day
Changing in every way
No Pharaohs of old
No tombs of gold
Just beggars cold
On streets of old.

Marlon Regan (8)
Grangewood Independent School

MODERN EGYPT

Egypt is modern
not ancient anymore.
It is changing
day by day
in almost every way.
From countryside,
to the big city.
The people go,
why? I don't know.

Harpal Bamrah (8)
Grangewood Independent School

WESTERN PRINCE

We've been hit!
Up on the first deck now Max!
Lifeboat No 3 please!
Yes sir!
Move out of my way!
Oh no! Lifeboat No 3 is at the bow.
Finally!

Take us down!
Row! One! Two! Three! Row . . .
Row back a bit, for the captain.
Beep . . . beep . . . beep.
You just heard the captain's last words.
Keep together now!
Try and keep with the other boats as well.
Shush! It's a German U-boat.
Flick . . . They took a picture of us.
I thought he was going to use the machine gun!
I saw something! . . . I can't!
I see it! I see it!
It's another liner.
Row nearer it and set off some flares.
I think they're going to rescue us . . .
I hope they don't hit us . . .
Climb up the rope ladders!
Don't worry Mr Peach! We'll pull you up.
Everyone on deck! Yes.
Can I see the captain! Yes! Right, I'll go up there.

Liam O'Sullivan (9)
Grangewood Independent School

AUTUMN LEAVES

Circling leaves golden and brown
Twisting and turning
Scampering down

Rushing wind, pushy and strong
Whistling and sighing
Driving along

Crowdy clouds, grey pencil sky
Laughing and playing
Bunching by

Sweet-voiced birds gathering for flight
Chirping and preening
Looking for sunlight

Whirling smoke, thoughts of fire
Blowing and puffing
Cover the spires

Falling rose scattered to earth
Drying and fading
Awaits new birth.

Adaora Inyama (8)
Grangewood Independent School

A VICTORIAN POEM

I live in a back-to-back house
My dreams will never come true
I wish I lived in a mansion
Like rich people do.

I wear ragged clothes
Clean chimney tops and roads
My family lives in the cellar
Like the rest on the roads.

Cydney Loughrey (8)
Grangewood Independent School

DON'T WASTE TIME

Got to do my homework
Got to brush my teeth
All to be done by half past eight
All to be complete.

Mum shouts, 'Don't waste time.'
I say, 'I'm not!'
Mum says, 'Have you done your homework?'
I say, 'No!'

Got to have my breakfast
But I want to have a sleep.
Got to have my morning wash
But I haven't brushed my teeth.

The moral to this poem
Is easy to understand.
'Ronell, don't waste time'.
'Mum, I'm not!'

Ronell Rochester (9)
Grangewood Independent School

Our Galaxy

Our galaxy
is full of stars
with lots of planets
one of them is Mars.

On dark nights
the milky way shines
looking like
a row of lines.

When the sun
shows its face
the milky way
flees from space.

Kiell Smith-Bynoe (9)
Grangewood Independent School

The Stars

Stars shine
in the sky.
They cling
together in
galaxies so high.
Many stars
lying in the space
twinkle and sprinkle
their light
over the night.

Sannan Khan (8)
Grangewood Independent School

VICTORIA

Queen Victoria our noble Queen.
She wore long frilly dresses out
and in.
When Albert her husband died
she was hardly seen.
Some people wondered
where she has been.

Mourning for her dear Albert.
She wore black instead of
colours such as blue, white or green.

Today her statue can be seen
in front of Buckingham Palace.
In loving memory of
Victoria our noble Queen.

Karen Sehmbi (9)
Grangewood Independent School

STARS

On dark nights stars flash.
On dark nights stars twinkle.
On dark nights stars look upon you.
On dark nights stars do a show in the sky.
On dark nights stars dance.
On dark nights stars prance.
On dark nights stars hop.
Until at last they stop.

Marcus Nurse (9)
Grangewood Independent School

A BAD TIME

Wherever I go there is a prison
To me,
Right here, right now.
What I say, what I do;
'I won't do anything for you.'

I may have a gun,
But I have never shot
Anyone.
People, people
What shall I do?
Shall I surrender,
Or shall I *shoot!*

Citizens and kids,
I am going to shoot one of you,
So please surrender.
Time is going slow!
Time has stopped!
What's the matter
With the time? But
First, I'm going to *shoot!*

Lady! Lady! Give me your
Money. Give me more
Of your money.
Why am I covered in handcuffs?
And why is there a net over me?
Why is everywhere a prison
To me?

Shahid Zaman (9)
Grangewood Independent School

ROAD OF TIME

(Slowly) Tick, tock, tick, tock.
           I can't see anything.
           Tick, tock, tick, tock.
           There is nothing in sight,
           On this endless road of time.

(Faster)   Tick, tock, tick, tock.
           The road is getting longer,
           Much longer.
           Tick, tock, tick, tock.
           The road is hot and dry,
           It's in a dusty desert.

(Faster)   Tick, tock, tick, tock.
           The path is hot and rocky,
           For it's made of time.
           Tick, tock, tick, tock.
           The desert's getting hotter
           And I am slowing down.

(Faster)   Tick, tock, tick, tock.
           I must keep on going,
           But the road is getting longer.
           Tick, tock, tick, tock.
(Slowly) The time is going by,
           On this endless road of time.

(Slower) Tick, tock, tick, tock.
           I am getting tired
           And time is going on.
           Tick, tock, tick, tock.
           I must keep on going,
           For time is . . . travelling on.

Martin Eden (10)
Grangewood Independent School

THE AUTUMN WIND

Where is the wind?
I do not know
But I can see it there,
in the swaying trees,
that blow in the breeze
and lose their leaves.

Where is the wind?
I do not know
But I can hear it there
as it whistles past my ears,
while I collect conkers on the ground.

Where is the wind?
I do not know
But I can feel it there
as it leaves
its icy fingerprints on
my face.

Where is the wind?
I think I know
It's outside
everywhere
I go!

Danielle Roberts (8)
Grangewood Independent School

MODERN EGYPT

Modern Egypt is new,
Old Egypt has gone,
Ended now,
New Egypt's reign has begun.

Everything is new,
'Graved - old' Egypt,
People don't want you,
Old Egypt has gone,
Modern Egypt reigns,
Old Egypt is only found in picture frames.

James Harris (8)
Grangewood Independent School

CHANGING EGYPT

Back then, big blocks
with no cement.
But now,
cranes, machinery!
Egypt has changed.

Back then, Pharaohs
and Lords.
But now President Mubareck rules.
Sorry, Rameses! No come back for you!

Back then camels
and donkeys.
But now,
cars, lorries,
the transport has even changed!

Back then little houses
like huts.
But now,
even they're gone.
What is Egypt coming to

By the way, what happened to the camels?

Esien Inyama (9)
Grangewood Independent School

TIME WAITS FOR NO ONE

'Time wait for me!
Can I catch up?
Will I catch up?
Why don't you have a rest?'

'Time wait for me!
How do you move that fast?
How do you keep going?
Let me catch up!'

'Time wait for me!
'You catch up!' shouts the clock.
'I can't!' I yell back
Should I catch up?
Would I catch up?
When will I catch up?
You're just too fast for me!'

'Time wait for me!
You can have a cup of tea!
Shall I catch up?
Will I catch up?
I'm not sure . . .'

'But won't you wait for me?'

Charlie Fisher (9)
Grangewood Independent School

TIME HEALS ALL WOUNDS

I was a happy child
When I was two.
Didn't worry about what I was to eat,
What I was to do.

My mum was pretty with short, straight hair.
It was as gold as the sun itself.
Her eyes were like sapphires
And a smile that would make the world stare.

When I was five
My mother died.
I wish she was alive.
Onto my mum's body I did dive.

The coffin was brown and polished.
The name plate shone.
There were loads of flowers
And also tears too.

When I was twenty-two
I had a child of my own.
When she asked about her grandmother
I said 'I didn't know.'

I then forgot about all the pain
And visited my mum's grave
Nearly every day.
It was then that I found that
Time heals all wounds.

Jolene Day (11)
Grangewood Independent School

THE WESTERN PRINCE

I'm on my way to Canada,
Away from this dreadful war.
So many people have died,
And I can't bear it any more.

So I packed my bags and suitcases,
And I'm on this massive liner.
The weather's nice,
So nothing could be finer.

Until one hour,
Whilst eating cake,
A torpedo hit us,
Which made us all shake.

The liner was sinking quickly,
So I got into a lifeboat,
People fell in with life-jackets on,
Luckily they could float.

We were rowing to shore,
In the freezing cold,
I had to row,
So I acted very bold.

Another liner came towards us,
But we managed to get away.
We saw a German submarine,
'This must be our unlucky day!'

Fortunately they didn't shoot us,
But I saw a flash of light,
I thought they were going to shoot us,
So I got quite a fright.

A ship passed by,
And gave us some oil,
To calm the sea down,
There's a war on so there isn't time to toil.

People died of hypothermia,
So on I had to go,
With people on top of me,
I still had to row.

Jamie Fisher (10)
Grangewood Independent School

I WAS SICK AND I WAS ILL

I was sick and I was ill
And I had to take my daily pill
When I took my daily pill
I wanted to do a cartwheel
I was nasty and I was mean
So I didn't make it on my football team.

When I was walking home from school
It started pouring down with rain
Then I went completely insane.

That is why I'm ill today
Because I spent too long playing in the rain.

Rikki St John (11)
Guardian Angels School

WITCHES

Witches, witches
brewing a spell,
frogs' legs, bats' wings,
what a smell!

Witches, witches,
they make such a fuss,
they don't have to be perfect,
like you and us.

Mixing the cauldron
1, 2, 3,
what shall we add now?
A plastic knee!

Joy Knowles (11)
Guardian Angels School

SPIKE'S NIKE

Spike was a boy that loved his toys
And always loved to wear Nike.
His favourite make he would never mistake
Even if it was on a bike.
His bike was Nike.
His hat and coat were Nike.
Everything in his life was
Nike, Nike, Nike.

Maxine Mullan (11)
Guardian Angels School

FRIENDS

Friends are loving,
Friends are caring,
Friends never leave you when you're hurt,
Friends are with you all the time,
Friends are with you day by day,
True friends anyway.

Friends are kind,
Friends don't mind,
To play with you when you're alone,
Friends you can depend on,
They'll never let you down,
Friends forgive you,
Friends don't moan.

Laura Gray (9)
Guardian Angels School

THE WORLD

The world is full of crime.
War, killing, what's the fuss?
People crying for some help,
Where's the civilisation and trust?
The world is full of hate,
Why can't we have a debate?
My mind is full of sadness,
I'm on the verge of madness.

Venus Urmatam (10)
Guardian Angels School

TIGER TIGER POEM

Tiger, tiger burning bright,
Send your love with might.
All the people on the Earth
Used to say that you were dirt.
But now I think you're burning bright.
I would say, some people shoot and kill you,
I think that's really sad.
I love you tigers, please don't die.
I don't like people wearing your skin,
All they want is to look supreme.
Tiger, tiger burning bright,
Send your love with all your might.

Donna Calleja (11)
Guardian Angels School

THE ALIEN!

As I was going to school today
I saw a spaceship and I said 'Wey hey!'
A three-legged alien jumped out of the ship,
He had a gigantic plastic hip.

I said 'Hello', he said 'Bha-bha.'
I said 'Do you live quite far?'
He said 'Lat-cat' then I saw his mac,
I chopped of his head and there he was
Dead!

Tylishia Green (10)
Guardian Angels School

WHATEVER GOES ON IN SCHOOL?

Whenever we go home from school,
We tell our mums we went to the pool.
But when we go to our rooms and get changed,
We tell our brothers and sisters the true story
In a whole different range.
Whenever we do science my friend Jo,
Bursts out of the room 'cause he needs to go.
When we started history my friend Fred whispered to me,
'Our teacher's old, know what I heard, she's 1003!'
When we were doing English we were studying slang,
But in room 33 they were doing science,
And an explosion began!
When we were doing maths we were doing divide,
But my friend didn't have a clue about it
So he copied mine!
Last but not least something happened to me,
I couldn't climb the rope 'cause I needed to go and pee.
Now it comes to an end,
Now you know what happens in my school,
And it's totally round the bend!

J J Facunla (11)
Guardian Angels School

MY NINTENDO 64

Control pad is super.
It's part of a wicked machine.
The graphics are great.
I'll give it 1,000,000 out of 1,000,000.
It's the best control pad I've played with.
I'm getting really addicted to it.
I can't wait until I get a new game.

Hayder Feely (10)
Guardian Angels School

KANGAROO

Kangaroo, kangaroo
What makes you
Bounce?
Is it the Australian sun
Oh can't you have some fun in the sun?
Or is it what you eat?
Kangaroo, kangaroo
Can you teach me how to
Bounce?
Oh stop playing with that lousy mouse
Are you listening to me?
Kangaroo, kangaroo, kangaroo.

Emmanuel Okorodudu (11)
Guardian Angels School

SKATING

Fast
Slow
Jump
Spin
Mind I don't crash in the bin.
Drift
Turn
Bounce
Win
When I'm skating I like to sing.

Steven Bush (10)
Guardian Angels School

WEEKEND

My weekend was fun
My weekend was cool
I stayed round my nan's
because there was no school!

For my breakfast
I had bacon and eggs
and I threw it at
my sister Meg!

On the Sunday
I stayed in bed
I couldn't get up
or lift my head!

Late that night
I went to bed
so all you need to know
has been said!

Jack Curd (10)
Guardian Angels School

CHILDREN BORN IN MAY

Children born in gentle May
smile like the shining sun.
They've lots of friends and give
their love to almost anyone.
The birthstone is the deepest
green, it keeps bad things away.
A happy life goes on
and on like one long holiday.

Aleishia Wilson (10)
Guardian Angels School

My Shadow

My shadow is very dark
My shadow is very big
and also very scary.
When I wake to morning light
my shadow has come.
But when night falls I go to sleep with
my shadow so dark beside me.
I leave my shadow to go to sleep.
It follows me for the next whole day
and while I do my work in school it
copies me with whatever I do.

Emma Jayne Smiley (10)
Guardian Angels School

Traffic

Beep beep!
Beep beep!
Get out of the way
Cars bumper to bumper
Horns honking all day.

Stinking like a garbage dump
Losing their temper
Fed up with stopping at red lights
Oh my gosh it's a bump.

Antira Jones (10)
Guardian Angels School

Rainbow

I can see a rainbow as bright as it can be.
Brighter than a star, brighter than a bee.

I can touch a rainbow, feels like a golden star.
It's not sticky one little bit, it's definitely not tar.

I can hear a rainbow, sounds like the voice of birds.
Not like the thumping noise of buffaloes in herds.

I can taste a rainbow, tastes like French toast.
Definitely doesn't taste like turkey on the roast.

I can smell a rainbow, smells as sweet as a rose.
It doesn't smell of dirty water from high-powered hose.

Wayne Jones (10)
Guardian Angels School

Friend

Someone to play with you
Listen to you
Be kind to you
Go around to their house
Share
Help you
Someone to talk to
Friendly.

Kirsty Shaw (9)
Guardian Angels School

Racism

Racists are mad
Their place is in prison
It doesn't matter whether you are black or white
Or even Asian
Most know here as home
This is their country
So don't abuse them
Or upset them
They're as human
As you and me
Even if they come from
Another country
They're part of the British family.
So you see
Racists are mad.

William Moore (10)
Gwyn Jones Primary School

Monkeys

Monkeys swing
Grip with their tails
they swing from tree to tree
scream very loud.
They swing with their tails
stop them from falling
they swing and play
they are calling
with their friends
Play and swing
all day long
from morn to dawn.

Veronica Fayers (10)
Gwyn Jones Primary School

SAVE OUR PLANET

The end of the world is coming near,
Save our planet we need it here.

Trees are being cut down,
No peace and quiet can be found.

The seas are being polluted,
The air is becoming black.
The rainforest is becoming,
Our enormous snack.

The Earth is becoming warmer.
We are living in it.
The Earth is dying away,
Bit by bit.

The end of the world is coming near,
Save our planet we need it here.

Shabana Buth (10)
Gwyn Jones Primary School

ANIMALS

Animals' homes in the rainforest
In the rainforest
Their homes are the best
So leave the trees alone
Don't just think about yourself
Think about the tribes
Rare trees and plants
They could cure some disease
Animals most important
They have lives too.

Shran Plaha (10)
Gwyn Jones Primary School

WHAT A DISMAL DAY

Raindrops dripping off the windowsill
falling on a cat outside.
What a dismal day. A tramp across the road
moving further into his sleeping bag.
The rain multiplies.
What a dismal day.
Pigeons huddle together on a roof top
keeping warm as the dismal day grows colder.
It's a terribly dismal day.
The day turns to night so quickly.
That was
a dismal day.

Melissa Wellings (11)
Gwyn Jones Primary School

RAINFORESTS

R uined
A nimals being killed
I t's cruel
N ative people live there
F or wood and money
O nce there were a lot of trees
R ainforests are important
E xtinct animals
S ome plants haven't been discovered yet
T rees being cut down
S ave the rainforests.

Philomena Lines (10)
Gwyn Jones Primary School

I Wonder Why

I wonder why
The tigers are nearly all gone
I wonder why
I wonder why.

I wonder why
There are such things as guns
I wonder why
I wonder why.

I wonder why
The whales are whining
I wonder why
I wonder why.

I wonder why
Most of the animals are dying
I wonder why
I wonder why.

I wonder why
There aren't many trees
I wonder why
I wonder why.

Save the rainforest please.

Hannah Preedy (10)
Gwyn Jones Primary School

SADNESS

Michael was his name,
he was my friend
until we went away.
Jerry was his name,
he was my teacher
I really wanted to stay.

But with all the guns
and the knives,
we wouldn't survive
in the violence
of our town.
We're going away,
there's nothing
to say
for sadness I
have found.

Ashur Lapompe (10)
Gwyn Jones Primary School

ANIMALS

It's   A trocious
A   N imals getting killed
         I   s it a game?
So   M e people think it is
         A nimals should live
         L et them
Plea S e!

Amil Ourabah (10)
Gwyn Jones Primary School

THE COSMIC POEM

Earth, Earth spins around,
spins around without a sound.
Mars, Mars very delicious but
no one lives there who is vicious.
Saturn, Saturn which has a ring,
unfortunately it has not got a king.
The Moon, the Moon it goes around
the Sun and the Earth every day.
I don't think so, no way!
Jupiter, Jupiter the biggest about,
that's for sure, there is no doubt.
Pluto, Pluto may be the smallest
which means it's definitely not the tallest.
Neptune, Neptune just about medium,
it would have been better if it had a comedian.

Rahmin
Halley Primary School

LITTLE EARTH

Hello I am Earth.
Lovely, colourful, marvellous Earth.
I am very dry because the nasty,
strong, terrible Sun dries me up.
I hurt sometimes when the scary,
awful, angry meteorites hit me.
I need some water because the Sun
is making me weaker and weaker.
The ocean gives me some water,
not all the time.
I don't have many friends because
the planets seem very far from me.

Papiu (7)
Halley Primary School

THE MOON POEM

Terrible, boiling, huge Sun.
Bright, shiny, yellow Moon.
Saturn is like a frisbee.
The gravity is like a magnet.
Mars is like an apple.
Hello I am Moon. I am having
the sun for my lunch like
a bun with a spoon.
I have a bun, round like a sun,
going round and round.
The clouds in the sky are like
some cream rolling around
an apple pie.
The stars are around the Sun
like a golden glass of water.
Marvellous, beautiful, wonderful Moon.
Vampire, rusty, scary Mars.

Kawsar Hussain (8)
Halley Primary School

THINGS IN SPACE

The Sun is like a bright bun.
The Moon is like a rune.
Jupiter is like me, big and strong.
A rock hits him on the head
and it doesn't hurt.
The bright light looks after me.
The Earth is like a bright ball and
Mars is like a dusty tomato.

Juman Ali
Halley Primary School

COSMIC POEM

This world is a giant marble,
a glassy rock rolling round and round but
if you see a cloud and if you kick it
your foot will go right through.
The equator around the earth
is a flexible frisbee.
Around the earth there are some clouds,
they are made out of ghost milk.
In my pocket there is a picture of a rocket.
The rocket goes up in the sky.
Do you know why?
To see a moon with a spoon
eating up the sun like a delicious bun.

Farha Nazmin (7)
Halley Primary School

LUNCH IN THE SUN

A Sun is like an orange that shines in the sky.
The Sun, the Sun gives us light!
When the Sun goes down, the Moon comes up.
The Moon is sometimes like a banana.
Hello my name is Pluto.
Black, white, colourful Earth.
Vampire, rusty, scary Mars.
Wonderful, bright shiny stars.
The Earth is like a marble.
I'm having lunch,
A bun with some sun.

Ataur Rahman (8)
Halley Primary School

MY FANTASTIC COSMOS

Safe, lonely, poor, silvery Moon.
Terrible, boiling, gigantic Sun.
Enormous, flaming and cold star.
Delicious, tasty, sugary Mars.
Smooth, fabulous, warm Earth.

Satellites, how wonderful you are.
People go to the Moon, do you see them?
A person once went and walked on it,
did you see him?
Christopher Columbus is a man,
do you know him?
He's a bit like Neil Armstrong.
Each one of them made an
amazing journey in my fantastic cosmos.

Samina Lipi (7)
Halley Primary School

THE SUN AND THE EARTH

Hello my name is the Sun.
I'm very, very hot because I'm a ball of gas.
I've almost got no friends because I'm too hot.
The Earth always talks to me.
He's the only friend I've got.
I like the Earth, he's good to me.
I am lucky that I've got a special friend.
The Earth is my very best friend.

Luke Pace (7)
Halley Primary School

THE RAIN

I don't care
what you say
I like the rain.
I like it when it
drifts on my
window-pane.

I don't care
what you say
I like the rain.
I like it when it's muddy
down the lane.

I don't care
what you say
I like the rain.
I like the silver
drops on my head.

I don't care
what you say
I like the rain.
I like the splash
of the rain.

I don't care
what you say
I like the rain.
I like the drizzle
of some on my
doorstep.

Farzana Begum (10)
Harry Gosling School

REMEMBERING YOU

Remembering you
A rainbow across the sky
With those colours
Which catches my eyes,
A spring flower with its
Lovely petals, reminds me
Of you every minute and hour,
I will remember you every time
I saw a wonderful coloured flower
In the middle of the sky.

In the middle of the dream, I saw
You and when I woke up, I
Saw a black shadow of you
In the garden,
I ran out and saw it was
Just a shadow.

Whenever I see your shadows,
The sunsets fades away, so
I never saw you again.

Shajida Rahman (9)
Harry Gosling School

RIVER COLSENDIN

'Young boy where have you been?'

'Went out fishing in the River Colsendin
and you know what I have seen?

A big long fish with ten fingers and two toes,
it looked like an eel but what could it be?'

'Who knows?'

'Young boy who was it you went fishing with?'
'No one just me, with a tuna tin.'

'Young boy, it could have been me you have seen
I went swimming in the River Colsendin.'

Shuba Begum (10)
Harry Gosling School

LIVING IN THE EAST OF LONDON

Living in the east of London
In the east of where
in the east of a dump
Squashed as a bundle of
rubbish.
With car pollution blowing
away the fresh air.
Noisy people with babies
crying.
Screaming like a group
of monkeys.
People shopping in different
kinds of places.
When can I ever get some
peace?
Never is the answer.

Nasreen Sultana (9)
Harry Gosling School

THE RAIN

I don't care what you say
I like
The rain.
I like it falling like tears
On the stony
Lane.

I don't care what you say
I like
The rain.
So I can go out and leave
My brother at home who
Is a pain.

I don't care what you say
I like
The rain.
That makes the farmers rush for their houses
And leave the wet
Grain.

I don't care what you say
I like
The rain.
I don't like the lane,
Too plain without the
Rain.

I don't care what you say
I like
The rain.
Trickling down
Along my spine
Tingling me
Making me
Shiver shiver shiver.

Shahidul Islam (10)
Harry Gosling School

SUDDEN MONSTER

Shadows on the wall,
Noises down the hall,
I'm not frightened at all.

It seems to be very scary,
I was very hungry.
I found a little cherry,
I started eating it,
Someone at my back grabbed me.

I looked back,
It was an ugly monster.
It ran behind me faster and faster.
The monster roared.
I looked around,
And found a sword on the ground.

I chopped the monster's head off,
The monster laid dead.
I straightaway went home,
And straightaway I went to bed.

Nilupa Yasmin (9)
Harry Gosling School

TRAVELLING TO THE MOON

I am going to the moon
Soon I will be on the moon
My rocket blasted off, boom, boom
I am getting closer and closer
I am getting interested, interested
I am ten inches away from the moon, inches
At last I am on the moon, at last
It is fun, great fun
It's home time, I have to go home now
Wait till next year
I am going to the sun
It will be fun, very great fun
Would you like to go to the moon or the sun?
I would.

Jaheduz Zaman (10)
Harry Gosling School

THE RAIN

I don't care what you say.
I like the rain pouring on
my window-pane.

I don't care what you say.
I like the puddles
that the rain makes.

I don't care what you say
I'm going out in the rain.

I like the noise
that the rain makes when
it drops on my boots.

Khaleda Hoque (9)
Harry Gosling School

ON THE WAY TO MARE STREET

'Come on Hakim, don't walk slow'
'Look Monic's taking a photo of an old house.' *Click!*
A dog barking and howling *woof, woof.*
'Look at the bent pole Nathania'
I hope I can make it on time
'Look, this time Miss Heap's taking
a photo of a clean house.' *Click!*
brum, brum, brum.
'You are slow Daniel.'
'Can I take a photo of those bones?'
'OK' said Pru
'Monic, take a photo of the Hackney Empire.'

Hakim Abdul (9)
London Fields Primary School

MY TRIP HOME

Brm, brm, brmm!
'Did you have an enjoyable day Ella?'
When I get home I'm going to bed.

Brm, brm, brmm!
My friends are waving to me
As I stepped into the car.
When I get home I'm going to bed.

Brm, brm, brmm!
People starting their cars to go home like us,
When I get home I'm going to bed.

Ella Flemyng (9)
London Fields Primary School

A WALK TO MARE STREET

I want to have a burger.
'We looked at the ancient church.'
I want to have a burger.
There were trees in the garden
and outside the garden
were a load of buildings.
I want to have a burger
'Wow look at that,'
cars making a noise like
bru, bru, bru!
I want to have a burger.
'Is that huge building old or new?'
I want to have a burger.

Joe Ngo (9)
London Fields Primary School

ON MY WAY TO BUTLINS

Butlins is going to be great.
'Leon get your head from the window.'
I heard nattering on the train.
'Leon get your head from the window.'
I gaze at the beautiful yellow cornfield.
'Leon get your head from the window.'
I wonder if there is going to be a fair.
'Leon get your head from the window.'
Look at the aeroplane taking off.
'Leon what did I say?'
'Get your head from the window.'
'Well do it!'

Leon Dunkley (9)
London Fields Primary School

THE LINE

'Mmmm I smell KFC.'
'Amy come on we are supposed
to be at the front of the line.'
Gossiping, muttering and chattering.
'Amy hurry up!'
Gossiping, muttering and chattering.
'Amy!'
'OK, OK, I'm coming, I'm coming.'

Amy Williams (9)
London Fields Primary School

I HATE

I hate school,
It's so boring,
All you're doing is sitting and learning.
I hate maths, I hate English,
Maths is boring, English I can't do,
But PE,
Well we'll see.

I hate my brother,
He's so annoying,
Please someone help me ignore him.

I hate soap, I hate baths,
Boy I'd never laugh,
After a bath you're so shiny,
But after I play footie,
Baths are like a strong wind and a monsoon,
But oh no! My bath is soon!

Thomas Phillips (11)
Nelson Primary School

THE WILD JUNGLE

The falcon flies through the bluest sky,
The tall giraffe walks proudly by.

The lion roars to show it's king,
And an eagle spreads its wide wing.

The monkeys chatter in the trees
The butterfly floats on a light breeze.

The hippos bathe in slimy mud,
And the elephant walks with a huge thud.

All is quiet and the sun goes down,
The animals sleep without a sound.

Kirsty Riches (10)
Nelson Primary School

THE CHEETAH

This hunter has a gift,
he is strong and he is swift.

With spots at his side,
which he wears with pride.

He stalks with pure skill,
ready to pounce for the kill.

The fastest animal on the ground,
a better hunter than a hound.

It can leap several metres in a single bound,
in the African Savannah where it is found.

Karan Murugavel (11)
Nelson Primary School

THE WOBBLY TOOTH

Once I had a wobbly tooth,
and it was such a pain.
I had to tell my mum,
that it was driving me insane.
I knew that this tooth
would never budge
so I tried to:
Rub and scrub, scrub, scrub.
Oh well, it's not going to budge
scratching my head,
I said to my mum,
'Please can you help me?'
Of course she said 'No.'
So if you have a wobbly tooth

Leave
      it
           well
                  alone!

Sophia Charles (10)
Nelson Primary School

THE COUNTRY

C is for clouds that float high above,
O is for the oak trees growing big and strong,
U is for undergrowth where the insects roam,
N is for the nightingale that sings so sweet,
T is for tulips that grow in the spring,
R is for running across the fields afar,
Y is for the yellow sun so warm and bright.
      If only I lived in the country.

Sarah Main (11)
Nelson Primary School

CLUCKY

I've got a chicken called Clucky,
He lays eggs everyday,
But the month he lays about ten eggs
Is probably June or May.
He lives in a barnyard
With other animals too,
The duck goes 'quack, quack, quack, quack!'
And the cow just goes 'mooooo!'
One day I took Clucky
To my primary school,
Everybody laughed at me
I felt like a fool.
Now my chicken Clucky
Is about 5 years old,
Every day of winter
Poor Clucky has a cold.

Tina Muman (11)
Nelson Primary School

VOLCANO

On an island.
The ground started to shake.
At first they thought it was an earthquake.
But then they knew it was the volcano.
The top looked like a tin of soup.
Then ash flew out.
People started to run.
Lava came down the volcano.
Burning everything in its path.
Children crying.

Daniel Pearce (10)
Nelson Primary School

ASSEMBLY BLUES

Class time,
Little time left,
Assembly time,
Scared, very scared,
Slowly walk outside.

Apparatus in the corner,
Starting the assembly,
Smiling parents watching,
Evacuation first,
My turn soon,
Blitz and armed forces,
Leaning on my desk again,
Yawning as we get back to work.

Sean M Greene (11)
Nelson Primary School

NATURE

Nature's beautiful,
Nature's sweet,
Nature's full of birds and trees.

Nature's clean,
Nature's green,
Nature's the most
Beautiful thing ever to be seen.

Nature's growing all the time,
I wish it was all mine.

Rejini Pradeepkumar (11)
Nelson Primary School

School

Reading, writing and arithmetic
All the time it makes me sick.

Multiplying, adding and take away,
Length and angles everyday.

Writing long stories and poems that rhyme,
But to write we have a limited time.

After lunch it's quiet reading
The only sound is of people breathing.

As quick as lightning the teacher's there
Behind her big brown desk on her wooden chair.

She stands up in front of the class
And speaks some gobbledegook really fast.

Half-past three on Friday
Going home by car or bus
I bet the teachers will be glad
To get rid of us.

Raabia Laher (10)
Nelson Primary School

Silly Teachers

S trict and moany,
I n the class,
L ovely and sweet with staff,
L ate at night,
Y es that's right.

T ime and time they get worse,
E ating like three monkeys in a purse,
A nd they,
C hew like frogs,
H ate it when we miss play,
E ating is hard because we have to pay,
R emember always,
S illy teachers get away.

Farida Khanam (11)
Nelson Primary School

MY LITTLE KITTY

My little kitty runs about
but when he gets sleepy he goes into a pout
His name is Jasper
he's my little friend
We'll stay together till the bitter end.

He loves to get in the washing machine
he hides in the airing cupboard
where the clothes are nice and clean
He is the *cutest* kitty
you've ever *seen!*

He loves cuddles with us all
but when he is not careful
he tends to fall
He climbs up the curtains
and brings them down
My dad doesn't like the things he does
He loves to play, he loves to pounce
he scratches but I don't care
he's my little pal!

Siobhan O'Brien (11)
Nelson Primary School

I'M FEELING A LITTLE SAD

I'm feeling a little sad,
It's time for me to go.
Now I'm not a little lad,
It's time for me to grow.

I'll miss the Nelson playground,
And all the fun and noise.
It's time to play with computers,
Not lots of little toys.

I'm going onto things that are new,
Although new friends I will find.
But in Nelson I feel nice and safe,
With all the teachers that are kind.

A very big fish in a very small sea,
That's how Nelson seems.
A tiny fish in a very big sea,
That's how Langdon will be.

So now it's almost time to leave,
So goodbye dear Nelson School.
Time to go to another place,
And learn every new rule.

So now you know why I'm sad,
It's time to leave this place I've known.
So goodbye dear old Nelson School,
The school I've outgrown.

Billy Evans (11)
Nelson Primary School

IN THE DARK

I am sitting in the dark
on my bed
waiting for my mum.

I am sitting in the dark
waiting in the living room
waiting for my dad.

I am sitting in the dark
on the toilet
waiting for my sister.

I am standing in the dark
waiting outside
waiting for my brother.

I am standing outside
still waiting
for my mum.

Still I am standing outside
waiting for my dad.

> *Gosh I am still waiting*
> *for them all!*

Lauren Champkins (10)
Nelson Primary School

COLOURS

White is here and there.
Yellow is the sun's shine.
Pink is the colour of a pale rose.
Orange is pure as orange juice.
Red is the blazing fire.
Green is laying grass.
Purple is going crazy.
Light blue is the sky and clouds.
Navy blue is rich and selfish.
Brown is the soggy soil.
Black is misty and dark to end all colours.

Raminder Kaur (9)
Nelson Primary School

COLOURS

Yellow is the colour of the sun
that fits in the sky like a puzzle.

Blue is the colour of the sea
that thrashes big waves.
When it starts to rain
the rain falls into the blue sea
and makes even bigger waves.

Red is the colour of blood
which happens when you cut yourself.
When you cut yourself again
it feels like you are going to die.

Lisa Perrett (9)
Olga Primary School

BAD DAY

My reflection in the mirror is ugly
Hot lava is oozing out of my eyes
My hammer in my head is annoying
Devils dance around me
Black, hell, real bad
My face is red
With all claws down it.

It goes quiet

My face is back to normal
The devils disappear
The blackness goes
My hammer in my head has stopped
My eyes are no longer oozing.

    Let's hope tomorrow
    Will be a better day.

Emma Brown (11)
Olga Primary School

ONE WICKED WITCH

One wicked witch went to Washington
Two terrorists terrorised Tower Bridge
Three frogs had a fruit party.
Four fidgety fleas flew for their friends
Five thin fools were flicked to the fields.
Six seals swam to the shore.
Seven sick sailors sailed to safety.
Eight elegant eels ate enormous apes.
Nine nuisance knots nattered.
Ten tall topless tins tilted over the river.

Charlotte Wright (10)
Olga Primary School

EMPTY

Where are you?
Hello,
anybody there?

Where are you hiding?
I want to get on.
School is for work.

They can't have gone
on a trip,
no.

Why are the pencils left out,
books still open
holders empty?

It's lunchtime.
No bell,
playground's empty.

Where's the food?
It's not laid out.
The hall isn't ready.
All vanished,
not there,
Gone.

Elizabeth Bollan (10)
Olga Primary School

BLACK

Black is the colour of a misty night.
Black is the colour of bats and
Black is the colour of a spooky forest.

Claire Happe (9)
Olga Primary School

DESCRIBING ANGER

It is like a parasite.
                Clinging onto me.
Although I cannot see it.
                It is an infected wound
                a scar, a burn.
A blindingly red-hot
heat.
                But the worst thing is.
You know it wants it.
                You know you want it.
And it will only be a
matter of time before
that beast breaks out
of its cage of blood and
bone.
                And then you are in
                its power.
A mad beast fuelled
by rage.
            Forever.

Tom Kora (10)
Olga Primary School

BLUE

Cold and wet,
Icy shores,
Wind blowing at your doors,
Rivers stop flowing,
Ice starts glowing,
Winter falls that day,
Warm animals come to play.

Jamie Blanks (9)
Olga Primary School

AUTUMN

Lost in a family of trees
They tower in over me
Stars glimmer like sparks from a fire
Kicking through the tall grass
The cool breeze tickles my face
The rain falls like pebbles
Birds chirp as loud as church bells
Crisp autumn leaves fall slowly to the ground.

Ian Coan & Ryan Wood (11)
Olga Primary School

GOLD

Gold is the colour of happiness
Bright, pretty as can be.
It shines in your eyes,
I can feel it strongly.

Libby Sherman (8)
Olga Primary School

PINK

Pink is nice.
Pink is spice.
Pink is light.
Pink doesn't fight.
Pink lips, pink cheeks.
Pink roses, pink posies.
Pink nails, pink snails.
Pink is at a bend
So this is the *end.*

Sarah Oak (8)
Olga Primary School

BILLY THE BULLY

I'm in the playground with nothing to do.
I see Billy who is the bully.
He's beating someone up and I get a
picture in my head.
Him doing the same thing to me.
I feel frightened and I wish that the feeling
would go away.
I feel like I'm in a desert.
No one to play with.
No one to talk to.
Just me alone, feeling unhappy and upset.
Then the picture goes away and I see
Billy coming up to me.
I try to scream, I try to run,
but I couldn't go anywhere because
Billy is getting closer to me.

Roxanna Spencer (10)
Olga Primary School

BLUE

Blue is the colour of the sea.
And the sky, light as you can see.
It's a peaceful colour to everyone.
Where you can have lots of fun.
Shivers start when winter comes.
Icy rivers, blue as you know.
Freezing people with blue faces,
Love's the colour blue.

Debbie Lantsbury (9)
Olga Primary School

COLOURS

Green

Green is the colour of the grass.
Green is the colour of springtime leaves,
and green is the colour of a stalk of a flower.

White

White is the colour of the just settled snow.
White is the colour of clouds
on a summer's day.

Blue

Blue is the colour of the sea.
Blue is the colour of the sky
in the day.

Ella Alder (9)
Olga Primary School

THE WIND

The wind is strong
and blows everything about,
Like a whirlpool
It blows men's hats away
and turns ladies' umbrellas inside out.
There's a child floating away
with a bunch of balloons,
while her mum was left
on the ground shouting.

Stacey Burton (7)
Olga Primary School

BULLIED

I've been bullied
it made me cry,
it made me lonely
I wanted to hide.
'Why pick on me
I've done nothing wrong,'
I was just playing,
doing no harm.
My mum would go mad!
When she'd see the marks
on my face,
the bruises on my arms, my legs,
any place.
It's not nice to be a bully, Mum says
and I know she is right,
My world would be much better
if there was not a bully in sight.

Ria Joseph (9)
Olga Primary School

ANGER

My head is erupting like a fiery volcano.
A chain saw is going through my throat.
My mind is about to explode,
explode with lost words.
My face goes red,
red as devils in the night sky.

Laura Quinton (11)
Olga Primary School

TEACHERS

I've got a teacher who's got funky hair
I also have a teacher who nobody can bear
I have a teacher who's got 4 ear-rings on each ear
Who drinks 20 gallons of beer every year.
I have a teacher who smells of cheese
who stinks, has warts and is amazingly big.
I have a teacher who I called a fool
and now I've been expelled from school.

Aklilu Teweldemedhin (11)
Olga Primary School

THE JUNGLE PLAYGROUND

I'm in the jungle playground,
little monkeys run about.
I'm in the jungle playground,
big snakes slither about.
I'm in the jungle playground,
a huge lion searching for flesh.
I'm in the jungle playground,
what a big mess.

Aaron Jordan (10)
Olga Primary School

BABY

Babies' bums all soft and round,
Pink, powdered and fluffily towelled.
Bottles, bibs and carrycots,
Flying potatoes and carrot tops!
Ointment, cream, bunny rabbit dreams,
Candyfloss and lots of screams!

Holly Samson (10)
Olga Primary School

WHAT MY SKELETON DOES

My skeleton can jump,
My skeleton can nod,
And wave.
It allows me to say 'No,' talk, fall and trip.
I can dance and prance and stand in a stance,
And then it will dance again.
The bone that is funny is the funny bone,
And the bone that holds the main computer
Is the skull.
The skull is egg-shaped
With three big holes,
But not as big as three small bowls.
My ribs are built as a cage
And connected to the spine,
Which holds the pelvis in place
And has the legs on too.
The arms stick onto the rib cage,
The hands are on the end
So this is what my skeleton is.

Alexander Reid (11)
Nightingale Primary School

WAR

Disconsolate men who stamp their
drenched boots.
Men with faces as vicious as a
mountain flying with lava.
Their strangled faces look up to the
red, bloody sky.
Bullets flying as men drop down
like a flock of birds
Lifeless bodies lying around.
When will they ever learn?

Ola Akinrele (11)
Rushmore Primary School

WAR POEM

My eyes open,
My left ankle aching like hell,
My eyes burning like fire,
Aahhh!
A mine explodes.
I try to crawl to the nearest trench,
My ears dying from the deafening screams,
I try to stand up,
I'll make it
Boom!
Everything goes silent,
Everyone is dead.

Patrick Flowers (11)
Rushmore Primary School

WAR POEM

We're all gonna die
blood dripping down our faces,
terrified people crying for us.
I wonder how it will feel to die?
Guns are shooting like fire
there's nobody there to help you.
Their faces are no longer alive.
Guns are exploding side to side.
People are dying,
no one cares.
I wonder how it will feel to die?
Up there in Heaven,
will I be panicking?
Nobody knows.
I wonder how it will feel to die?
They say in our religion
that if we are bad
God will put us in fire.
If we're good we will get gold gifts,
shining and dropping down.
I wonder how it will feel to die?

Hinna Wadiwala (11)
Rushmore Primary School

WAR POEM

Pale faces bobbing up and down.
The muddy trenches hold victims
of blood and betrayal.
The air is dense for sweat
is all around.
The deafening sound of
gunfire holds it all.
Dead men all around,
but nobody cares,
nobody!
A deafening cry, and a screech
asks us 'Why, why is there war?'

Kieron Donovan (11)
Rushmore Primary School

ELECTRICITY

E lectricity is helpful, I think you would agree,
L ines and cables behind the wall, where you can't see.
E lectricity is dangerous, electric shocks it makes,
C ables behind the wall, don't light the birthday cake.
T ime to go to bed, turn off the light,
R ight down the stairs the lamp's still bright.
I nteresting electricity, well what more could you want,
C omputers, lots of them with writing changing font,
I ntriguing pylons way up high,
T ilting wires, cars zooming by.
Y o, that's electricity.

Daniel Servante (9)
Rushmore Primary School

It's Hallowe'en

Trick or treat is on the way
For Hallowe'en starts today.

It's time to scream
It's time to run
For the monsters
Are out
To have some *Fun!*

Witches fly across the sky
Making the kids scream and cry.

The trick or treaters are worn out
Now their mothers give them a shout

    'Bedtime!'

Ruby Silverlock (9)
Rushmore Primary School

Animals

I love ants
But they're always in my pants
I love ants.

I love bees
But they're always on my knees
I love bees.

I love cats
But they're always wetting mats
I love cats.

I love dogs
But they're always chewing logs
I love dogs.

Roxanne Apps (9)
Rushmore Primary School

IN MY BOX

In my box
I put . . .
all dirty, smelly socks,
slimy food,
nasty mucky windows.

In my box
I put . . .
bad people,
evil men and women,
things that hurt.

In my box
I put
terrifying, ugly doors,
revolting books that scare people.

My box is made of . . .
Metal chain and wood,
I will send my box
underground in a cupboard,
and put the key in the sea.

Alice Barton (9)
Rushmore Primary School

OUT IN THE FIELD . . .

Out in the field on a rainy Sunday night,
I heard a crazy wolf howling,
A noisy dog barking,
A silly cat purring.

Out in the field on a cold Monday night,
I saw a rabbit sniffing,
A snake slithering,
An adult sleeping.

Out in the field on a stormy Tuesday night,
I smelt a bonfire burning,
A slimy space rat,
Some blooming flowers.

Out in the field on a wintry Wednesday night,
I felt rubbing rain,
A bracing breeze,
Some dripping icicles.

Out in the field on a shining Thursday night,
I heard buzzing homeward bees,
Sisters arguing,
Brainy bullies fighting.

Out in the field on a sleepy Friday night,
I saw a giant's chair,
A red pond,
A Frisbee tree.

Out in the field on a long Saturday night,
I fell asleep . . .

Sophie Shnapp (9)
Rushmore Primary School

THE HARVEST MAN

The old ancient harvest man visited me,
As he walked with his golden leafy hair,
Crackling, crunching the fallen leaves.

Collecting crops crackling like the wind,
His leaves drift off him quietly,
In our playground he became grumpy.
Suddenly, crackle, crackle, crackle.

He shrunk smaller each second,
And as it happened I said 'Good riddance.'

Matthew Ting (10)
St Agnes RC Primary School

WATCHING TV ON A SUNDAY ABOUT DIANA

Watching TV on Sunday
Was very sad
It gave me a knock
And a bit of a shock
For 24 hours go past
On the clock
And she is still dead
What a feeling for her boys.
A pat on the head reminds them of the dead
Memories brought back time and time again.

Charelle Modeste (10)
St Agnes RC Primary School

HARVEST TIME

The harvest is a nice person
He gathers food and fruit to have festivals
He dresses in all different types of leaves
His arms and legs are twigs
His eyes are bright
He comes every autumn and walks on crispy crunchy leaves.
He smiles like a bright blossom
His ears are the shape of a rose
The harvest brings out the sunshine
He is as pretty as flowers
His hair is golden wheat.

Jordan John (11)
St Agnes RC Primary School

RAINFOREST RHYTHMS

The heavenly smell of the rainforest
The rustling of the trees
The natural green browns and blinding reds
The tropical taste of the fruit
The fresh dripping juice dripping down your mouth
Now dawn is gone
Not it's dusk
The howling
The hooting
The roaring of the lions
Dawn has come, time to start my day again.

Tendayi Jimbere (11)
St Agnes RC Primary School

SUMMER CALYPSO

The coconut tree looks out across the tropical sea,
the steel band is on its way.
Smell that ripe plantain frying in the sizzling pan.
It's a bright, hot, scorching summer's day.
Summer calypso singing in the boiling sun
and the children they eat till the day is done.
The children they eat the watermelon sweet,
The steel band begins to play.
Smell that cooked plantain better if you taste it,
it's a bright hot scorching summer's day.
Summer calypso singing in the boiling sun
and the children they eat till the day is done.

Natalie Mathurin (11)
St Agnes RC Primary School

A CHANGE IN LIFE

At first it seems so dead and dreary
The roots come out
It's looking weary.

Growing, growing, growing
It's beautiful
The green's showing.

But now we're in the middle of spring
The blossoms blossomed
And it begins to sing.

Dean Nevill (11)
St Agnes RC Primary School

A HAUNTED HOUSE

I walked up to the haunted house,
Opened the door and crept in like a mouse,
The squeak of the stairs, the screech of the door,
The thud of the footstep on the wooden floor,
The hoot of an owl in a tree so bare,
My heart pounds as I climb the stair,
The tick of the clock,
The howl of the wind,
The thunder, the lightning,
The distant light dimmed,
The bedroom ahead of me, the duvet turned down,
Undressing so quickly not making a sound
Under the clothes hidden so deep
The haunted house vanishes, lost in my sleep.

Louise Leahy (11)
St Agnes RC Primary School

RAINFOREST

Rainforest, rainforest with rattling trees
The birds are singing
Water drips from the leaves
Insects are crawling
Monkeys are swinging
Birds come past you
Bringing joy to your ears.

Rainforest, rainforest
I wish I was there now
I'd go home with a feeling of fresh, damp air.

Paul Andrew (10)
St Agnes RC Primary School

Caribbean Calypso

I'm going to the Caribbean
Not the coliseum
Flying fish
Is a national dish
There are steel bands
Playing in the golden sand

Palm trees swing in the breeze
While you sit and listen at ease
This moonlit night we sit in the sand
Gazing to sea hand in hand
Tomorrow I go home
But not alone
Calypso dance
Sends me into a trance
I moan because
I have to go home to Rome.

Catherine Phillips (11)
St Agnes RC Primary School

Refreshing Moments

I is for ice-cream all frosty and cool,
C is for chocolate delicious with all,
E is for extras, how long should I wait?
C is for choice, I love them all,
R is for refreshing and also rich,
E is for eating it out of a dish,
A is for almonds sprinkled around,
M is for moments, how pleasurable it sounds.

Kelly Welch (11)
St Agnes RC Primary School

THE HAUNTED HOUSE

As I entered the haunted house,
The place was all, as quiet as a mouse,
The sights I saw were tremendously scary,
When all of a sudden, something hairy,
Oh! It was nothing, just an old broom,
Creeping out of the dusty room,
All you could see was dust, dust, dust,
And in the far corner, a small lurking gust,
When all of a sudden, the house became alive.

With noises here and everywhere,
I felt cold and very bare,
I thought to myself 'This ain't fair!'
Where there was once a broom became a boo!
Where there was once a gust became an ooogh!
When all of a sudden, the broom began to fly,
I couldn't believe it, it was right up high,
I stepped right back and headed for the door,
When just like this the broom fell to the floor,
Just after that it became worse and worse,
I thought to myself 'This house is a curse!'
I left at that minute and headed for home,
To which I call my shining dome!

Iddanella Baumbast (11)
St Agnes RC Primary School

THE STRONG WIND

The wind blasted into the room,
It wasn't soft, it was like a big *boom!*
He twisted and whirled,
He struggled and twirled.
Howling like a wolf in the night
Bullying the windows but never in sight.
But then all of a sudden,
He came up to me,
Battered and untidy
Not forgetting the word straggly.
But then for some reason
He drifted away,
Quiet as a mouse
And nothing to say.

Sam Watts (11)
St Agnes RC Primary School

CARIBBEAN EXPERIENCES

The Caribbean is a colourful place,
St Lucia the place to be.
So why not try St Lucia.
Experience the sights,
Experience the sea,
Experience how happy you can be.
Taste the plantain,
Taste the coconut,
Watch the steel bands play,
The Caribbean is a colourful place.
St Lucia is the place to be.
So why not try St Lucia.
Experience the sights,
Experience the sea,
Experience how happy you can be.

Natasha Lavery (11)
St Agnes RC Primary School

THE RAINFOREST

The squawk of the birds wakes all
And the bellow of the roaring lions terrorises
The crunch of the rich vegetation crackles under our feet
The hues of the extraordinary fruits are magnificent
And the tint and intelligence of the creatures shows
Plants so dazzling, all so very sturdy
On the impressive ground wild creatures roam
Howling, hooting and scratching noises pervade the air
While fierce cheetahs ramble everywhere.

Sean Griffin (11)
St Agnes RC Primary School

THE SCARECROW

She has a body of straw
which is messy and tatty
her job
to keep the birds away
as she stays still as quiet as a mouse
with nobody to talk to
and nobody comes to see her
not even the farmer
he just walks past
and acts like she isn't there
every time she hears the crunching, crumbling corn
she thinks somebody is coming to see her
but then the farmer just walks by making the corn
crunch and crumble
as the birds pick at her straw
the farmer makes crunching, crumbling
noises as he walks through the corn then
the birds just fly away.

Joanne Flaherty (11)
St Agnes RC Primary School

HECTIC DAY

It was a Christmas gathering that snowy night
My sister and I were having a fight
Mum came upstairs and gave us a fright
Dad came in and said he was fired
He touched his legs and said he was tired.
We sat down, had a cup of coffee
Mum shared between us a box of toffee
I would never go back in time to that day.

Neville Wandera (11)
St Antony's RC Junior School, Forest Gate

CHOCOLATE

Chocolate chocolate good to eat,
Chocolate chocolate a delicious treat.
You can eat it with a friend,
You can eat it to the end,
Chocolate chocolate good to eat.

Chocolate chocolate dark and white,
Chocolate chocolate I'll take a bite.
You can get it from the superstore,
You can get it from Mr Barrymore,
Chocolate chocolate dark and white.

Chocolate chocolate big and small,
Chocolate chocolate I'll take it all,
You can eat it with a Kit-Kat,
You can eat it with a knick-knack,
Chocolate chocolate big and small.

Jonathan Barquilla (11)
St Antony's RC Junior School, Forest Gate

RECYCLE

All around us are things to recycle,
Like plastic, paper, shoes and textiles,
We could have another chance,
To make the world a better place and dance.

The world would be a greater place,
With recycled things in front of our face,
People would be much happier,
If people recycled instead of the bin.

Janet Castro (10)
St Antony's RC Junior School, Forest Gate

MY FRIEND

My friend is always fancy
She always likes to read,
But sometimes is very moany,
When it comes to sowing some seeds.

I don't like the way she is now,
She still acts the same,
When it comes to reading time,
Guess what she does again?

She's sometimes very annoying,
Unfortunately no one cares,
When it comes to playtime,
She always pulls my hair.

I don't think she's a good friend to me,
Because of what she's done,
Every time she's bothering me,
When it's time to run.

Karizza Torres (10)
St Antony's RC Junior School, Forest Gate

THE BIG STORM

Thunder clashing.
Lightning flashing high up in the sky.
The wind is whirling round and round,
While the hail stones come by.

There are puddles everywhere.
All the sky is bare.
There's darkness in the air.

Laura Robinson (9)
St Antony's RC Junior School, Forest Gate

SCHOOL IS COOL... AS IF

School is cool . . . As if . . . It's boring and really stupid.
You should just skip it
Like I did!
The teacher'd seem a hundred years old
Most of them are fat and bald.
They seem to go on about nothing and nothing.
And what was our homework?
Write something about something.
I'll tell you something even worse
It's horrid I tell you!
School dinners!
They are iccky and yucky
And taste like a dead mouse.
The peas taste strange, kind of like a woodlouse.

Another thing I hate
Are the stupid things we learn
Such as the zero times tables.
We go over them a hundred times
Yet still get them wrong.
We hate singing songs which tell us to pity
Teachers hardly sung by preachers.
Our uniforms are even worse.
When I have to wear them it's like a curse.
We really hate going swimming
For all we wear are little socks
And if we're lucky little frocks.
The rules are really dumb.
There's one when we have to suck our thumbs.
Our school is really nutty
They make us go really batty.
So school is cool right . . . As if.

Amanda Rose Casela (11)
St Antony's RC Junior School, Forest Gate

THE EVIL WITCH

There was once an evil witch,
she lived in a damp, dark ditch.
She ate a mouldy lump of crogslime,
and swallowed it down with a lump of frogslime.
Her brain was left in a dusty room,
where it came to its sad, sad doom.
The witch said it's time for bed,
and tried to do away with our heads.

Theresa Akintunde (10)
St Antony's RC Junior School, Forest Gate

MY COMPUTER HAS BUGS

My computer has bugs
And they go glug glug glug
They chew my computer
Until nothing is left.

Sarah-Louise Augustin (10)
St Antony's RC Junior School, Forest Gate

GRENDEL

Grendel's eyes are green and glowing,
Grendel's nails are red and sharp,
Grendel's face is always mean,
Grendel's teeth are very pointed,
Grendel's breath is like a sewer.

Ray Mierau (7)
St Antony's RC Junior School, Forest Gate

JUNGLE

In the jungle there is always some kind of tangle,
Monkeys swinging from tree to tree
Just how it should be.
The lion is the king, searches for food
As long as it's good, but the lion doesn't
Worry about the rest, and he knows he's the best.
Animals like to keep together at the end of the day,
They don't care what the human says because the
Jungle forever is how it will stay.

Bruno Camacho (10)
St Antony's RC Junior School, Forest Gate

DAY DREAMS

Miss Fuller thinks I am reading
But I'm on the moon floating like a boat.
Looking at the stars
And on my way to Mars.
Miss Fuller thinks I'm listening
But I'm in the future
I'm looking at how cars will be.
Miss Fuller thinks I'm working
But I've gone inside a magic land
To see all kinds of magic
I see a cat flying in the air
I see water disappear from a glass
And I see a person sawed in half
Miss Fuller thinks I'm reading
And this
Time she's right.

Eva Owusu-Ansah (11)
St Antony's RC Junior School, Forest Gate

WHAT'S THE MEANING?

'What's the true meaning?' I asked my mum,
'Is it puddings and sweets to fill your tum?'
'Of course not' she answered in a huff.
'It's about sharing and giving and lots of love.'

'What's the true meaning?' I asked my dad,
'Is it toys and games which makes you glad?'
'Of course not' he answered in a stare,
'It's about loving and happiness and a dash of care.'

'What's the true meaning?' I asked myself.
'I know we share all our wealth.
We share and give thanks for our good health,
That means no meat!'

Lewis Iwu (11)
St Antony's RC Junior School, Forest Gate

WHAT'S BEHIND THE STAFF ROOM DOOR?

What's behind the staff room door?
There could be old coffee stains on the floor.
Lots of teachers, unmarked books and
Naughty children hanging on hooks.
Scrambled eggs spread around the floor
And hungry teachers asking for more.
Private secrets carved on wall
While the light on the ceiling's bound to fall.
Toe nails floating in cold cups of tea and
Oh look the staff room door's about to fall
On me!

Anna Vernon (10)
St Antony's RC Junior School, Forest Gate

WITCHES' SPELL

Grumble, grumble the cauldron tumbles,
it sizzles and sizzles and bubbles and bubbles.

Guts of gorilla, eyelids of ape,
go in the cauldron and let it bake.

Grumble, grumble the cauldron tumbles,
it sizzles and sizzles and bubbles and bubbles.

Flames of candlelight run run run,
children are burnt down into the ground.

Grumble, grumble the cauldron tumbles,
it sizzles and sizzles and bubbles and bubbles.

Catherine Lovell (12)
St Antony's RC Junior School, Forest Gate

MY MAGIC LAND

In my magic land there would be,
Lots of sweets and presents for me.
A chocolate river, a milkshake lake,
Toffee trees and a giant cake.

Wouldn't it be nice to be,
Swimming in the deep blue sea,
With beautiful mermaids and giant whales,
Holding on to dolphins' tails.

But most of all I'd like to be,
Able to stay with my family,
So they could play and laugh with me,
Sharing my magic fantasy.

Leigh-Anne Defreitas (10)
St Antony's RC Junior School, Forest Gate

THE FROG SCHOOL

Twenty frogs come to the frog school.
Twenty frogs, green as the garden pool.
The lesson must start.

To three naughty frogs arriving late,
The teacher says, 'I can't wait.
So please take your places,
And show me your faces.
Don't fidget, don't wriggle, be good.'

One little frog dreams of the sunshine, of clouds, and the puddles
In springtime, of insects that buzz around lilies . . .
'You must pay attention,' snaps teacher.

Then when the lessons and learning are done,
It's time for the frogs to have fun.
They dive and they hop, they leap and they flop.
The water's alive with their games.

Jermaine Arthur (9)
St Antony's RC Junior School, Forest Gate

GRENDEL

Grendel is evil,
Grendel is mean,
Grendel is cruel,
Grendel is selfish,
Grendel can hear you,
Grendel can eat you,
Grendel can smell you a mile away,
He can hear you in the night,
Grendel can hear you crying in the night.

Nicole Smith (8)
St Antony's RC Junior School, Forest Gate

WEATHER

It's a battle between the wind and rain,
ice and snow fight again.
I don't know why they all fight,
because it's terrible when they use all their might.
Falling, rolling, tumbling, turning,
everything seems to be burning.
All because the wind and rain,
ice and snow fight again.
All you hear is thunder, lightning,
pouring rain and sudden fighting.
Thunder lashing, lightning flashing,
everybody can't get to sleep,
that's why I always weep on a winter's night.

Jade Stanley (9)
St Antony's RC Junior School, Forest Gate

THE WIND

The wind was howling
Through the night
The wind was
Puffing with all its
    Might.

The wind made the clouds
Turn grey
And it made all the
People say
'I wish it was another
    Day!'

Cheryl Braganza (9)
St Antony's RC Junior School, Forest Gate

WHAT I AM

I am what I am,
I love what I am,
You may not like what I am,
But, I cannot change what I am,
Because it is wonderful to be what I am,
God made me the way I am,
In his image, this is the way I am,
I am proud to be who I am,
I feel blessed and grateful to God for being what I am,
What I am, makes me feel very happy,
Be happy for me because I am,
Not different from what you are,
The only difference maybe is that you are what you are,
And I am what I am,
In God's eyes we are all the same,
And he loves us the way we are!

Munya Chidakwa (10)
St Antony's RC Junior School, Forest Gate

GRENDEL

Grendel is an evil snake monster,
You can hear bones crunching in his throat,
If you get in his way, you will get eaten up by him,
He has thick skin and if you try to kill him
It will not make a mark,
He is very scary,
And when he slithers he slithers slowly.

Alain Carver (8)
St Antony's RC Junior School, Forest Gate

THE ARGUMENT

One stormy winter night,
When me and mum had a fight,
All I wanted was for her to say,
That it was all right.
But all she said instead was 'Go to bed.'
I begged and begged inside my head,
For her to stay beside my bed.
The night seemed long,
Oh what a dread.
I thought I would confide in Ted.

Soraya Sackey (8)
St Antony's RC Junior School, Forest Gate

GOING TO AMERICA

At Easter I'm going to the
States, I cannot wait
Big cars
Movie stars
Hotels
Motels
Rich people
Poor people
Mickey Mouse
The White House
Space rockets
Lots of chocolates
Back on a plane
Home again.

Isabelle Sarley (9)
St Antony's RC Junior School, Forest Gate

GRENDEL THE MONSTER

Grendel's mean and his eyes are green,
His teeth are jagged and crooked,
His breath is so foul it would make you howl,
His skin is tough and scaly,
By day he sleeps in a bottomless lake,
By night he comes out and slithers like a snake,
He'll eat you before you can scream or shout,
No one can save you when Grendel's about!

Hannah Gilligan (8)
St Antony's RC Junior School, Forest Gate

MY BIRTHDAY

Me and my friend went out to tea,
We wriggled, we giggled and we smiled with glee.
My mum and my dad gave me presents on Monday,
But after Saturday I'm going to pray on Sunday.
When I got on my bike I was afraid I might fall,
But when I got the hang of it I felt ten feet tall.

Amber Charles (8)
St Antony's RC Junior School, Forest Gate

LENT

Lent is a time when you love *God* more.
Lent is a time when you do things you haven't done before.
Lent is a time when you give up your *sins*.
Lent is a time when you do new things . . .

Dawn Juckiewicz (9)
St Antony's RC Junior School, Forest Gate

HOMEWORK

I get homework every day,
Too much studying when I want to play.
No time to watch telly or even go out,
I must know my times tables or mum will shout.

Exhausted and tired from school I return,
When I look in my book, there are spellings to learn.
Another story to write, division sums too,
A whole day at school is enough to do.

After school we should be allowed to have fun,
To ride on our bikes and to play in the sun.
Practice makes perfect so I am told,
But I want some fun before I get old.

Hannah Matthews (8)
St Antony's RC Junior School, Forest Gate

MY SISTER

She is as sweet as sugar,
And I love her too,
She is as small as an acorn,
And I love her too,
She's as bold as she is old,
And I love her too,
She eats like a monster,
And I love her too,
She sleeps like an angel,
And she loves me too.

Michelle Browne (7)
St Antony's RC Junior School, Forest Gate

SAVE OUR WORLD

Have you ever stopped to think;
What our world would be like,
if life became extinct.

The trees and flowers all no more;
Making everything dull grey and a bore.

No animals running wild and about;
No fishes swimming in or out;
No birds flying in the sky;
All will be still, oh my! Oh my!

We must look after the world today
and make sure all life has a say;
The tiger, the elephant and the whale;
we need to preserve not grow pale.

Man is the world's most destructive force;
destroying forests, rivers, seas till they are really gross;
We must all act now to save our world.

James McDonald (10)
St Antony's RC Junior School, Forest Gate

NIGHT AND DAY

The night is dark,
The morning is light,
When we wake up,
I hope it is bright,
The night is dark,
The morning is light,
When we fall asleep,
I hope the stars are bright.

Quiana John Charles (8)
St Antony's RC Junior School, Forest Gate

CORY'S GORY STORY

There was once a gory story,
About a boy named Cory,
Cory lived with his sister Nory,
Who lived up on the tenth storey,
Cory's life would have been longer,
If it had not been for Mr Bonger,
Mr Bonger was very sorry,
When he ran over Cory with his lorry.

Patrick Akintunde (8)
St Antony's RC Junior School, Forest Gate

JACK'S CATS

A boy called Jack,
Had a big fat cat,
Jack's cat had four little ones,
Who always tried to steal mum's buns,
One day they were caught and got in trouble,
Jack's mum yelled out, 'Get out on the double.'

Ryan Dench (8)
St Antony's RC Junior School, Forest Gate

POEMS

P oems, you can read them when you're happy,
   you can read them when you're sad
O r you can read them before you go to bed
E veryone can read a poem, young or old
M ake yourself a poem, create yourself a poem.

Kristian Hamilton (10)
St Antony's RC Junior School, Forest Gate

SNOWY

My rabbit Snowy is all soft and fluffy.
She makes you feel all gentle and sweet inside
As I watch her munch on her sunburnt orange carrot
Then turn to watch a fierce dog
Just waiting to pounce.
'Go away' I say
And soon the fierce dog became a sad dog.

When it is about eight o'clock
I say 'Time for bed Snowy'
And I hold her in my arms
Until she
Falls asleep
Just like a lazy baby.

Samantha Auguste (10)
St Antony's RC Junior School, Forest Gate

SPRINGY HAIR

Hair so curly,
Springing round and round,
Up and down,
Twirling, whirling,
What fun it is to have,
Curly, whirly hair
Like a spring.

Rhian Joseph (7)
St Antony's RC Junior School, Forest Gate

WHAT I'D LIKE TO BE

I'd like to become a millionaire,
Or even the Prime Minister like Tony Blair.

But really I want to be a footballer,
Or swim in the sea like a scuba diver.

It would be brilliant to be the most richest king,
Or be in a band, so I can sing, sing, sing.

I'd like to be an astronaut,
So I can travel through space,
Or I could be in the Olympics,
And win every race.

For bronze, silver and gold medals would be quite ace,
But for now I like learning at my own pace.

Dwain Lucktung (10)
St Antony's RC Junior School, Forest Gate

GRENDEL THE MONSTER

Grendel is not very nice,
His skin is cracked and sore,
His eyes are green,
That is why he's so mean,
His breath is like a drain,
That is why he has no brain,
He comes out at night,
And gives everyone a fright,
His teeth are crooked and yellow,
That is why he's such an ugly fellow.

Simone Dominique (8)
St Antony's RC Junior School, Forest Gate

VICIOUS GRENDEL

Grendel the monster with his big green eyes,
He eats small people and doesn't like flies,
His skin is all scaly and his belly is fat,
He walks around and he thinks he's all that,
Nobody knows when he comes and when he goes,
The only signs that he lives are a trail of old bones.

Vanessa Laurent-Grant (8)
St Antony's RC Junior School, Forest Gate

I CAN'T FIND

I can't find my teddy
nor my shoes
I can't find my pretty
clothes
please help me
oh mummy, please help me
I just can't find anything.

Laeticia Bulambwe (10)
St Antony's RC Junior School, Forest Gate

TV

I love TV
I watch it excitedly,
And I know you'll like it a lot,
So why don't you get out of that cot!
You can watch comedies, cookery shows,
And even programmes for tips about clothes!

Jennifer Flanagan (10)
St Antony's RC Junior School, Forest Gate

MISS GRAY

My teacher's name is Miss Gray,
She is from Philadelphia in the US of A,
She has red hair,
Sometimes she is fair,
But if you step out of line,
She will give you a hard time,
I think she is quite nice,
I wonder if she eats easy to cook rice,
She swapped places with Mr Caddle who now
lives in the US of A,
This is my teacher Miss Gray.

Simon Labonte (9)
St Antony's RC Junior School, Forest Gate

MEAN GRENDEL

Grendel is mean,
His eyes are green,
His body is coiled,
And he should be boiled,
He is so strong,
But he looks all wrong,
His feet are big,
He looks like a pig,
He smells like a drain,
And when he flicks you, you feel great pain.

Antoinette Fontaine (8)
St Antony's RC Junior School, Forest Gate

Monday Is A Homework Day

Monday is a homework day, I kick
and scream till the end of May.
My mother told me off today
for screaming till the end of May.
My auntie said 'Stop shouting now
before I come over there and give
you a pow!'
I hate Mondays and homework.

Monique Clarke (10)
St Antony's RC Junior School, Forest Gate

School

Doing work every day
Set by our teacher Miss Gray
Maths, English, science too
With no help or even a clue
Working hard from a sheet too
We also use scissors, paper and PVA glue
Everyday we are sent to school
Even the good, bad and unlucky too.

Jonathan Loh (10)
St Antony's RC Junior School, Forest Gate

The Ghost Teacher

The school is closed, the children are gone,
But the ghost of the teacher lingers on.
As the daylight fades, as the daytime ends,
As the night draws in, she stands in the classroom, as clear as glass
And calls the names of her absent *class.*

Heather Djan (10)
St Antony's RC Junior School, Forest Gate

CARNIVAL TIME

Carnival time is the best time of the year.
People dance and drink beer.
Men and women wear their carnival clothes.
The clothes are bright.
People party all night.
Because carnival time is the best time of the year.

Marvin Nicholas (10)
St Antony's RC Junior School, Forest Gate

SWIMMING

Going swimming every day
And all my swimming instructors always say
'Faster Maria, faster
Before you drown in a disaster'
And before I get to the end
They've started once again
I got so angry by day and night
That I wanted to push them with all my might.

Maria Cavilla (10)
St Antony's RC Junior School, Forest Gate

AUTUMN

In autumn the trees are bare
Because the leaves are not there
They are lying on the ground
Where they can be found
In colours of red, yellow and brown
You see people raking them away from their door
So you can see the nice long path on the floor.

Zelda Prichard (9)
St Antony's RC Junior School, Forest Gate

Robots

They run on batteries and wires,
And they blow up in fires,
They look really cool,
And they always carry a spare tool.

They eat electricity and run around crazy,
They're machines so they're never lazy,
They drink warm sweet oil,
While their gadgets bubble and boil.

Jonathon Peirce (10)
St Antony's RC Junior School, Forest Gate

The Skipping Rope

I am a skipping rope smelly and old,
I lie alone smelly and cold,
The others hate me and say I'm weird,
They put me in puddles and leave me there,
When I'm dry I'm muddy in and out,
As I hear children shout and run about,
When break is over,
I'm tossed under and over,
And left alone with no one to talk to.

Kehinde Oyegunle (11)
St Antony's RC Junior School, Forest Gate

LIONESS

I'm a lioness who hunts at night.
I am trapped in a cage not even getting out.
No fresh meat to eat but raw, rotten meat.
No fresh water but sewer water.
No friends, no one to play with and laugh with.
Does it have to be this way?
I imagine that I could go back to
Africa to see my cubs and my family
And live my life to the fullest and see the
Sunrise and sunset.

Taiwo Oyegunle (11)
St Antony's RC Junior School, Forest Gate

I HATE FOOD

My name is Moany,
I want to be Boney.
I cannot do games,
I have to sit at the side,
While you call me names.
I hate fish and chips,
I prefer a packet of crisps.
So give me some money,
To buy some treats,
Like some *sweets*.

Angelique Roccia (11)
St Antony's RC Junior School, Forest Gate

MY LITTLE SISTER

My little sister is called Maria,
She has black curly hair.
She causes a lot of trouble for me,
But she doesn't seem to care.

I can't really call her little though,
She is quite big for her age.
She hates not to get her own way,
She should be locked up in a cage.

I do get on with my sister sometimes,
That part is kind of true.
I would miss her if she wasn't here,
There would be so much I couldn't do.

I wouldn't be able to play games with her,
It would be such a bore.
I will be nice to her this year,
This month she will be turning four.

Leanne Vele (10)
St Antony's RC Junior School, Forest Gate

THE BEAST

In the forest lurks the beast,
Its fiery red eyes glowing in the darkness.
Its fluffy tail moving side to side,
Its teeth long and sharp.
Its legs strong and agile,
Its body like a suit of armour.
Its claws sharp and deadly,
Its mind clever and cunning.

Nikal Jeyakumar (10)
St Antony's RC Junior School, Forest Gate

A Picturesque Journey

The day is coming to an end,
And the sun is setting slowly.
Docile and mellow,
Amber and rose.
Fiery yet soft, gentle and clear.
An enchanted glow that shines
And lights the street below
The colour of a scarlet berry
Or a sheaf of golden corn
Gradually it fades,
And night engulfs the day.
It's sable and shadowy,
Sullen and dusky.
Some cats assemble
As the sky turns ebony
Magic creeps upon us.
Suddenly the moon appears
A flicker of illumination
White and clear,
Sleek and lustrous.
It shines through the foliage
Lighting the way for auburn foxes
And prickly hedgehogs.
The world is silent
And the sky twinkles with stars.
It is quiet, as quiet
It turns chilly and melancholy.
Strangely overcast
Night is upon us!

Lucy Archibald (10)
St Joseph's Convent School, Wanstead

Autumn

Red and yellow, a pale blue sky
As autumn comes along
Summer says goodbye.
A crunch and a rustle
As I step upon the discarded
Horse chestnut shells.

Watch the drifting clouds
And smell that fresh air smell
Look at the leaves floating and whirling
And as they fall to the ground
Others start swirling.

The hedgehog and the squirrel
Must hibernate but why?
As autumn comes along
Summer says goodbye.

Melissa Fontaine (10)
St Joseph's Convent School, Wanstead,

As I Watched The Sun Go Down

I looked out of my bedroom window,
And saw the sun slip down.
A bird flew from a tree top,
Then there was darkness all around.

As the sun shone its last fingers at the sky,
I listened to the birds singing as they went by,
I heard a cat miaowing,
And a dog barking
And I also saw people eating their dinner and laughing.

The wind blew harder and harder,
As the sky grew darker and darker,
I saw a girl walk down my street, she
Was wrapped up warm from head to feet.

The sun had gone, the stars were out
And also the moon was about.
I went to bed at nine o'clock,
Ready to rise at eight o'clock.

Hayley Wong (11)
St Joseph's Convent School, Wanstead

A DIFFERENT SEASON

Air is cool and moist,
As I breathe in a breath of fresh autumn air,
While I watch the billowing, feathery clouds
As they float softly across the pale-blue sky.
I sit by the fire,
Just warming my hands,
A spider, it spins its web beside me,
And I cover my face and scream.
As I walk along the path,
Discarded shells of conkers and acorns
Crackle as I tread on them.
Squirrels scurry along, searching for fallen chestnuts,
As people take injured hedgehogs,
To the RSPCA.
Hear the birds migrating, from this,
To a warmer country.
The fragile autumn leaves, red, golden, brown,
Drop from the trees, floating, curling, twirling down.

Katie Lim (11)
St Joseph's Convent School, Wanstead

THE MORNING TO COME

The sun rises,
High in the sky.
The crow calls,
That morning has come.

The sun shines,
Bright and hot.
And birds twitter,
In shady spots.

The day grows shorter,
Afternoon comes in.
A choir of cats,
Start to make a din.

The sky begins to change,
As the sun goes down.
Red, orange, yellow, pink,
While the sun's rays shine out,
Like a delicate crown.

The moon twinkles,
The stars glitter.
As I pull up my covers,
I leave the day behind.
And think ahead,
Of the morning to come.

Maria Coyne (11)
St Joseph's Convent School, Wanstead

FIREWORKS NIGHT

The fireworks sparkle,
The bonfire glows,
The colours are gleaming
And everyone knows.

The babies all cry,
The children are fine,
The parents all watching
Keeping an eye on the time.

We all watch the fire,
Without one small sound,
Everyone stares and
Gathers around.

They're watching really closely
And gathering up
Everyone's holding a small
Plastic cup.

Time to go home now
All children weep
Back home they go
To fall fast asleep.

Brooke Kirby (11)
St Joseph's Convent School, Wanstead

URBAN LIFE

As I am waiting for the Ilford train,
I look about, nothing is plain,
There's not even a garden in a city, so bare,
But always an exciting alley somewhere.

I board the train and rush for a seat,
As the other passengers come as a fleet,
Out of the window a car flies by,
Disappearing into a tunnel as a plane soars high.

The screeching of wheels,
As the train grinds to a halt,
And the icy road is covered with salt.

The workmen wearing their bright yellow hats,
Working on scaffolding up the side of the flats.
The swishing and swooshing of a grimy road cleaner,
Holds up the traffic and makes drivers meaner.

The warm air as you pass an open shop door,
Makes you feel homely and want to buy more.
I force myself home for I've dinner to eat,
And at home are some friends I am dying to meet.

Francesca Le-Surf (10)
St Joseph's Convent School, Wanstead

URBAN LIFE

I've just turned the corner of Regent Street
That's where all the season shoppers meet
Double decker buses crowd the street
People get on to save their feet.

Roller shutters open wide,
Cash tills have money rolling in.
While the people are strolling,
Down the new spring Oxford Street.

Buses grinding to a halt
There's a traffic light fault.
Little kiosks on the pavement,
Drilling holes in the road.

Babies crying, children wanting
The toy that's the latest craze.
The latest sale is making a fortune
Because of the Neptune pearls.

Taxis crowd the street,
Waiting for clients needing a lift.
Market sellers yelling three for two
Two for the price of one.
It's always a bargain.

Alison Fernett (11)
St Joseph's Convent School, Wanstead

WHY?

I looked into the dark night sky
And wondered why oh why
Did Guy Fawkes have to die?

What did he do,
When the flames leaped high?
Why oh why did he die?
What did he do
When flames seized his waist
And curled around his neck?

He breathed his last breath
Before he dropped his head
All the people were silent
Because Guy Fawkes was dead.

Lily Elizabeth Jones (11)
St Joseph's Convent School, Wanstead

THE MAD RUSH

The sky is dark,
The sky is grey.
Women in long dresses try to find their way,
In the busy streets of London.
Smoke from the cars makes us choke and cough,
There are only two cyclists today.

I stand there looking about,
There's nothing but people around me.
The tall buildings tower over me,
Making me feel small.
I look at my watch, I was late again.
I needed to run, but where?

The sky opens.
It starts to rain.
Not very hard although.
Women cover over their buggies
Men put up umbrellas.
Children spin around in circles,
                in the cool wet rain.

I barge through the long wet street
Like a bull in a china shop.
Finally I see a zebra-crossing.
On the other side was my destination
The great big train station.
I cross the road, go inside.
Buy my ticket and make it just on time.

Victoria Jenna Jeffers (11)
St Joseph's Convent School, Wanstead

WANSTEAD

We're on our way to Wanstead, on the 101,
We're on our way to the cake shop to have a cream bun.
Mum's in Somerfield for the weekly shop,
I'll help her with the bags before she drops.
Now we're off to the park, Daniella sees a horse trit trot, trit trot,
                                                                       trit trot,
Its shining coat and mane, shining beautifully in the sun,
Makes me feel so happy that summer time has come!
We're on our way home, on the 101,
The cattle are coming, quick hide, no run!
They're nibbling at the hedges, eating all the grass,
Quick they've gone down our road and they might eat our roses.
If we're really good and eat all our tea,
Mum said we can feed the ducks on the pond.

Luisa Anne Katie Bonomo (11)
St Joseph's Convent School, Wanstead

CITY LIFE

The dark, bleak city town
Opens up before me.
A pigeon swoops down, down, down
On to the ground in front of me.

Crying babies in their prams,
Holding tight to toys with their little hands.
Mothers trying to keep control
Of their children
Envious of people who idly stroll.

Cars sending water, flying high
As they go racing by.
Splash!
A child is wet
The mother begins to fret.
'He'll die because of the flu
And he is only *two!*'

The car grinds to a stop
And is given a fine by a police cop.
'Two hundred pounds, pay right now.'
'I haven't got the money
I don't know how.'

Trains go rattling by
Dads rush to work
Still tying their tie.
Briefcases swinging from side to side
Most of them made from a dead cow's hide.

Samantha Coles (10)
St Joseph's Convent School, Wanstead

BONFIRE NIGHT

Coldy fingers
Coldy toes
Up in the sky
Another one goes.

Hats, scarves,
Jeans and jumper
People huddled
To gasp in wonder.

More sticks put on
The flames grow higher.
Sparks are flying
From the big bonfire.

Rockets, Catherine wheels
Lots of light.
More squeals
From the people
In the night.

The sky glows
From all the light
Red, green, orange and white -
Suddenly all is dark,
But up goes a colourful spark.

Olivia Jane Adshead (11)
St Joseph's Convent School, Wanstead

THE BUSY HIGH STREET

A crowded scene in the
  busy High Street,
Where babies cry and
  mothers meet.

Children are playing on
  the swings in the park,
While dogs run around
  and begin to bark.

People run about to
  catch their bus,
They're making a loud noise
  and a terrible fuss.

The sun goes in and
  the weather's cool,
A little boy's crying
  for he has lost his ball.

This is the scene of
  the busy High Street,
Where the babies cry
  and the mothers meet.

Clare Cubberley (11)
St Joseph's Convent School, Wanstead

CITY LIFE

When I turn round the corner
And I look left and right,
I saw a red Mercedes then
It went out of sight.
Then the bus went by
The conductor started talking,
'Tickets please,' he said
Then started walking.

Children shout
While I cross the street,
Babies cry
When the parents meet.
The phone starts ringing
The traffic begins,
The dog starts barking
While the milkman sings.

The drilling from the workmen
Is hurting my ears
Leaves start falling
Then there's children's cheers.
Then I turned round the corner
And I looked left and right,
I saw a red Mercedes
It was back in sight.

Judy Frimpong (10)
St Joseph's Convent School, Wanstead

CITY LIFE

As I look out of the window
I can see the dead sun,
Setting in the misty skies.
You can hear the trees,
Swaying in the night.
The dead sun rises
From behind the horizon.
Lighting the beautiful green fields.
People rush to the market square.
Pigeons swoop down from the tree tops.
Children ride their bikes really fast.
As they speed down the road
On their bikes,
They can feel the summer breeze
Brushing their faces.
You can see the children going into the library
You can hear the thunder of the trains
Rushing under the tunnel.
The dead sun sets
Back down into the horizon
While children are crying to go to bed
But there is still another day ahead.

Sémone Modeste (10)
St Joseph's Convent School, Wanstead

A NEW DAY

Crimson seeps through the velvet blanket
That wraps the world around,
Dew drops shining delicately
Twinkle on the ground.
Birds all join in chorus;
To welcome the king of day,
Daisies gaze in wonder;
He'd banished the night away!
The cheerful lambs in the fields do play
Whilst the ewes all stand together;
The old, brown cow lies on the green
Enjoying the humid weather.
The village children run back home
As four o'clock draws near;
The ancient church bells start to ring,
Loud and clear
When twilight falls the mysterious moon
Reveals her papery face,
The stars; her ladies in waiting,
Lower her veil of lace.

Adjoa Anyimadu (11)
St Joseph's Convent School, Wanstead

The Journey Throughout The Day

Out of the night,
Into the day.
In comes the light,
Shining away.

Away goes the sun,
Say goodbye.
Morning is done,
Afternoon will soon die.

No sign of light,
Not a single sound.
Here comes night,
Morning's coming around.

Yogeeta Chandegra (11)
St Joseph's Convent School, Wanstead

Cosmic

Cosmic, cosmic up so high.
I wish I could fly up so high
Up so high, it's out of this world
It's up in space where the space is clear.

In space there is something,
People call it *cosmic* rays
But no one cares to tell
So that's that for *cosmic* today . . .

Jo-Anna Mills (10)
St Luke's Primary School

COSMIC

Somewhere high up in the sky
There is a place where no one lives called space.

Space is dark with little light
Unlike the sun which is big and bright.

World, space, stars and all
Are cosmic you know, universal.

Charley Knight (10)
St Luke's Primary School

I WISH

I wish that I could live on the moon
And say hello to the stars,
I wish that I could fly so high
And visit the Sun and Mars.
I wish that I could be a bird
And see the world up so high,
I wish that I could be a bird
And let the world pass by.
Also I wish I could talk to dolphins
And for them to talk back to me.
But now I think I've wished for too much . . .
As you can see!

Claire Rattigan (11)
St Paul's with St Michael's Primary School

NIGHT

Night has appeared as black as coal
The moon now rises like a football
My world has moved
Now it's time for me
Restlessly animals awake
Hunting for their prey.

The moon now disappears into
A raging ball
The sun is a coin shining as gold
The world is a little ball
With people as small as us all
Now the gold coin flips over
The sun is no more.

Deroy De Bordes (11)
St Paul's with St Michael's Primary School

ANIMALS

The slimy snake
Slithers slowly to Southern California.
Sun shining on his scaly skin
And shedding it slowly as he slithers along
On the scorching sand
Stopping to stare for some sign of some supper
Silence, stillness,
'No supper in sight,' he sighs.

Grant Murphy (10)
St Paul's with St Michael's Primary School

SPACE SALAD

Space is like a gigantic, enormous kitchen with all the most scrumptious food in it. Full of wonder, delight and *food*.
Mouth watering Mars: The huge, tasty and squishy red tomato. Full of lovely red juice like red wine except much brighter and tastier.
Scrumptious Saturn: A glistening pineapple ring around a yummy, scrummy scoop of vanilla ice-cream. Every so often this planet has mouth watering and gigantic flood of fresh pineapple juice.
Very tasty Venus: This is one of the most adorable delights in space. It is one great big, soft, squishy ball of candyfloss. Like a planet full of mattresses. All the sugar going up the nose makes the person want to sing and dance.
Perfect Pluto: The teeny tiny, freezing cold ice-cube perched in space. There has never been a drought here because the luscious water is forever melting away off of the planet.
These are just some of the culinary delights you'll find in space so keep on searching.

Claire Scoresby-Barrow (10)
Salisbury Primary School

THE COSMIC PICTURE

Space like a black sheet of sugar paper straightened and flat.
A pinch of glitter for the stars, an opal and ruby for Neptune and Mars.
A pearly button for the moon, and the sun could be a polished
                                            Spanish doubloon.
A whoosh of talcum powder just before play, that gives the sugar paper
                                            the Milky Way.
Mixed up plasticine squashed down flat to make the Earth and
                                            now that's that.
My cosmic picture's over and done now I have to decide where it
                                            should be hung.

Kimberley Taylor (10)
Salisbury Primary School

THE PEOPLE'S PRINCESS

She became a princess
And bought us joy
To young and old
To sick and poor.
She bought happiness on her tours
She was bright, she was fun
She was known by everyone
One hot August night
She was a diminished light
Her death brought sadness to the world
To men, women, boys and girls.

Adeeba Azam (10)
Salisbury Primary School

SPACE

I sometimes wish to go out in space,
To see all the planets,
Mercury, Venus, Mars, Jupiter, Saturn, Neptune,
Pluto and the outside of our Earth.
I dream about it day and night
I sometimes got told off at school,
I can't concentrate in my best subject
And can't wake up in the morning.
When does school finish?
I don't know.
I just can't stop dreaming about it
But I do believe I will go there one day.

Nazmin Begum (10)
Salisbury Primary School

COOL ALIENS!

Cool Aliens appeared at my school
They came from outer space
They were green and hairy too
It scared me, would it scare you?
They talked a funny language
And didn't move out of their place.
Everybody laughed but not me.
Just then a hairy, green, slimy
Alien jumped high (he nearly touched the ceiling)
Took my teacher's dinner money
Oh no! I gasped
While my class giggled.

Vicky Patel (10)
Salisbury Primary School

SPRING

Spring is coming
Spring is here
Spring is a lovely time of a year
Flowers bloom
Birds sing
There is beauty in everything
The sun comes out shining bright
There's lots of stars in the night.

Farihaa Azam (11)
Salisbury Primary School

IN THE DARK SPACE

There was space
Thick and dark
There was the sun burning hard
The moon is showing to the planet Earth
The space is dark
As dark as dirt
The space is not a friendly dark
But there was only dark
You can't see
No trees
No water
No people
No food
No animals
Just space
Thick and dark.

Zahra Rammahi (10)
Salisbury Primary School

SPACE

I am floating in darkness
This darkness is space.
There are shooting stars passing
My face.
There are planets so dull,
And planets so bright.
There are some planets far away
Out of sight.
Oh and there are aliens in
Space ships what a fright.

Toni Goodwin (10)
Salisbury Primary School

WATERFALL

Waterfall, waterfall
Cold and noisy
Rushing down the mountain.

Rumbling, gushing
Fast and clean
Magnificently speeding.

Nothing better
Than watching
A waterfall.

Gallons and
Gallons of
Water gushing.

Look at that
Waterfall
never stopping.

Saliha Khansia (10)
Shaftesbury Primary School

WHAT IS WAR?

I see war everywhere
I see fires everywhere in houses.
I see children crying for their parents.
I see bombs falling all around us.
I see lights from fires and bombs.
I see buildings burning from high.
I see houses bombed.
I see people shocked and sad.

Jigna Bhadresa (10)
Shaftesbury Primary School

My Auntie Mary

My Auntie Mary
Is very big and hairy.
At night she acts so weird
She grows a very long beard.
She has a little pet
She keeps it in a net.
Her best friend is crazy
She is so lazy.
What else can I say about my Auntie Mary?
She's just so scary.

Raheen Saiyed (10)
Shaftesbury Primary School

Autumn

Something whispery, windy and wild,
Catches my ears twice.
Something crunchy falling down,
Oh it must be the leaves of autumn time.

Something tells me it's autumn
By the leaves crunching down,
Cold twisting swirling rain
Falling from the sky.

Brown, rustly, orange leaves
Falling from the trees,
Red day fills with little
Bits of yellow.
Bye, bye autumn, see you tomorrow.

Mahjabin Choudhury (10)
Shaftesbury Primary School

DON'T

Don't touch the fire
Don't touch the pig
Don't be a liar
Don't wear that wig.

Don't kick that telephone
Don't hit the cat
Don't blow that saxophone
Don't kick the bat.

Don't drink that glue
Don't open that tin
Don't paint that blue
Don't kick that bin.

Wahidur Rahman (9)
Shaftesbury Primary School

WATERFALL

The river is gushing and splashing
Going fast
Starting at the mountains
I don't think it will stop
Changing colours too good to watch
Bubbling and speeding down and down
Gushing and rushing very fast
Swishing and whooshing going down
Gallons of water
Shiny and glittering as it goes past
Clean and fresh falling heavily
Never stopping waterfall.

Sumera Saleem (11)
Shaftesbury Primary School

SEA TURTLES

Sea turtles are large, beautiful creatures,
That swim in the warm ocean.

Their nesting beaches are being destroyed,
And the sea turtles are very annoyed.

They are captured for their meat which is sold for food.
Some people eat them if they are in a mood.

Sea turtles' skin is made into leather.
People like to make their coat and wear it in cold weather.

Sometimes they like to come out in the sun.
Please don't kill them with your gun.

Zaira Bashir (10)
Shaftesbury Primary School

SUPER MUM

My mum is a super hero,
She can count backwards down to zero.
Wearing an apron at home, zooming around,
Super mum cannot be found!
She calls herself speed of light,
Travels too fast and gives me a fright.
All work is done in a minute,
She's the one who has no limit.
She tries her best to make everything perfect,
Wouldn't hurt a creature including an insect.
She's soft at heart and very tender,
Any mistakes and she will surrender.
Some of my friends call her dumb,
I'm proud that she's my *mum!*

Rita Roy (11)
Shaftesbury Primary School

WATERFALL POEM

The waterfall is rushing down
Very fast on to the rocks
The waterfall is very noisy and cold
The waterfall is clean and fresh
The waterfall splashes and spits if you stand close
The waterfall is very misty,
Might not be able to see anything
Whooshing and swishing, speeding downwards
Gallons of water
Bubbling changes colour
Sparkles when it hits the water
Never stops from the mountains
To the river.

Omran Tariq (11)
Shaftesbury Primary School

DON'T

Don't kick the cat
Don't lick the baboon
Don't sit on the dog
Don't burst the balloon.

Don't push the elephant
Don't drink the cola
Don't sit on the peacock
Don't take my hat.

Don't lie to me
Don't ride my bike on the ceiling
Don't poke me
Don't push my saxophone.

Minesh Kanzaria (10)
Shaftesbury Primary School

SECOND WORLD WAR

Lots of bombs falling
Whoosh, boom, bang
You never get enough
Sleep in the war.
There are bombs falling
Like heavy rain.

Machine guns sound
Like bashing thunder,
Soldiers try and try
But most of them
Just die and die.

There is too much war,
Please have no more
People say 'We want peace,
We will even beg on our knees.'

Please end the war
I wish it was against the law.

Sunny Pindoria (11)
Shaftesbury Primary School

LIFE IN WAR

Why can't this country have peace
So people can have a happy life?

As I look out of the window and I
See playing like nothing is happening but
Everything evil you can imagine is out there.

Suddenly the bombs fell
Like a load of exploding engines
And thunderous footballs.

The air raid siren wailed to say it was safe
And I went in the dark and dusky sky
To see people crying and some people dead.

Pritesh Sonigra (10)
Shaftesbury Primary School

WORLD WAR II

Bombs are exploding like
fireworks,
Aeroplanes zoom like
birds,
Houses are tearing apart
like pieces of paper.
Evacuees are leaving their
parents in terrible horror.
Bullets zooming in the sky
like a piece of metal thrown in the air.
Parents crying
Children hurting
When they go away.
Guns shooting, *shoot, shoot.*
shoot.
Killing people,
killing soldiers,
killing children
who didn't go away.

Navinderpal Chana (10)
Shaftesbury Primary School

I Should Have Stayed In Bed Today

I should have stayed in bed today,
In bed isn't where I belong,
As soon as I didn't get up today,
Things didn't start going wrong,
I got a splinter in my foot,
My puppy toy made me fall,
I squirted toothpaste in my nose,
I crashed into a wall.
I knocked my table off the glass,
But it didn't land on the floor.
I didn't spill a glass of chocolate milk,
It's soaking through my clothes,
I accidentally didn't bite my tongue,
That really made me moan,
I tickled my funny bone,
And it laughed all the day long.

Aliya Khatun (9)
Shaftesbury Primary School

World War II

Bombs falling down on the ground.
There is lots of rationing going on.
The bombs are footballs.

We hear bombs and guns.
Shooting, banging and cracking.
Children are scared of the war.

Children can hear bombs in the night.
Bombs are falling on cities like tennis balls.
Houses are bombed and scattered about.

Neetha Kaur (11)
Shaftesbury Primary School

POETRY CALENDAR

January:	Children build snowmen.
February:	Pretty flowers are dying.
March:	Say thank you to the special person on Mother's Day.
April:	Cold rain is coming
May:	Birds are hunting for food.
June:	Pretty flowers are growing
July:	Sunflowers reach to the sun
August:	People go to the beach and have a swim.
September:	Vegetables and fruit grow.
October:	All the leaves on the trees have fallen.
November:	All the festivals come.
December:	Cold and icy snow.

Mayuri Patel (10)
Shaftesbury Primary School

THE BLITZ

Bombs are landing,
Bombs are bombing in all countries,
People are suffering,
Sadness of people that are dying,
It shouldn't be happening,
Bomb, bomb the bombing,
Suddenly the blitz is ending,
Hooray, hooray! It has ended.
Will it ever happen again?

Sukhvinder Merway (11)
Shaftesbury Primary School

THE SILLY THINGS HE DOES

My brother does some silly things
You won't believe, guess what?
He bites his nails
And eats live snails, with ketchup, - baloney the lot!

When my mum's not at home, she's shopping
When I'm not at home, I'm at school.
But when my brother's not at home, he's spraying
The neighbour's garden with baby food, air freshener and glue!

My brother also collects worms,
A disgusting habit, you think
But then he squishes them up
And hides them under the sink
Then when my mum wants to wash
And no water comes out
She'll look under the sink,
And get a big stink
Then gives my brother a clout.

My brother is a real snitch
He tells of me to mum
He breaks the window on purpose
I think that is so dumb!

My brother does some silly things
You know, believe me, so there
I'm stuck with him for ever
So I'll never forget my prayer.

Sonia Bhatti (11)
Shaftesbury Primary School

THE BEAUTIFUL HYACINTH

The hyacinth gives a delicate fresh smell,
A beautiful colour, a tiny bell.

They twist and swirl in the gentle breeze,
Don't sniff too hard or you will sneeze.

In the season, spring, in the park they grow,
Neatly lined up in a straight row.

Its leaves are such a smooth green
In springtime the beautiful hyacinth is seen.

Amena Umer (11) & Amelia Chowdhury (11)
Shaftesbury Primary School

WAR

War is frightening,
War is awful,
War is hell,
And war is dreadful.

War makes people suffer,
War affects everyone.

World War One, gone
World War Two, gone.

War is haunting
War is powerful
War brings on emotion.

Usama Ihtasham (11)
Shaftesbury Primary School

THE MYSTERIOUS JUNGLE

When some of the animals are asleep
Other animals creep
When the weather is at its best
Most of the birds make their nests
When the rain pours
All the lions roar
When the weather is nice and sunny
Out come all the bunnies
When the birds sing
The bees can sting
When you hear the noise of the
                        rattling snake
All the animals suddenly awake
When the tiger is on a hunting chase
It catches its prey at a quick pace
At the crack of dawn
Most of the animals yawn.

Pritika Lal (11)
Shaftesbury Primar School

EVACUATION

I was evacuated,
Separated from my family.
It was a sad moment for me and the other children.
Some children even cried.
But I didn't cry.
There were tears dropping from my mum's eyes
Like rain falling.
As I waved goodbye to my mum a raindrop fell from my eye.

Hannah Zubir (10)
Shaftesbury Primary School

WAR

Why does war happen?
Why can't people live in peace?
Why do grown-ups fight
When they say it's silly to fight?
Can't they stop fighting
And taking people's lives?
Do they feel happy after
Tearing apart their families?
People are murdered,
Their houses are destroyed
And their lives are ruined.

Kauser Hussein (11)
Shaftesbury Primary School

THE EVACUATED CHILD

I'm happy but lonely
I miss my mum and dad
I hope that they are alright.
I'm safe but I would like to
Come home with my wonderful parents.
At night I'm wondering if
You're alright because there's no light.
When can I come home?
Because I love you lots and
I miss you too.

Karen Piekielniak (11)
Shaftesbury Primary School

THERE IS NO PEACE

Bombs are falling on the houses, like
Someone throwing hot metal balls down.
There is no peace.

People running around, like
Scared pigeons chased by men.
Children are not playing,
They are evacuated.
There is no peace.

Not enough food to feed,
Not much drink or proper shelter,
Plenty of injured people,
Not enough doctors,
There is no peace.

Children crying,
Leaving their parents behind,
Like a lost cub,
Looking for its mother,
There is no peace.

Sayeeda Hossain (11)
Shaftesbury Primary School

AUTUMN

The brown, red and golden leaves fall from trees.
The leaves in the park all fall on the ground.
The leaves sometimes change colour in autumn.
The wind shakes the trees and the leaves fall down.
Autumn, autumn I do not like you.
Goodnight autumn and good morning winter.

Rajeepan Loganathan (9)
Shaftesbury Primary School

LIVERPOOL FC

Liverpool on top,
Replacing the Kop,
Tonight is the big match.
Here we go, kick-off time,
Hope James keeps them out until full-time.
Fowler running, passing, dribbling
Owen with a cross.
Should be a goal!
Fowler scores,
Flowers thrown
And it's full-time
With no added on time.
One-nil! One-nil!

Viren Patel (11)
Shaftesbury Primary School

WAR POEM

Why did we have war?
Why not peace?
Bombs dropping
Houses exploding.

Children sad, separated
from mum and dad
Rationing of food

Crying all the way
in the train
hearing bombs in the night.

Why did we have war?

Arif Amin (10)
Shaftesbury Primary School

COLOURS

Green is for grass, thin and long.
Green is for a tank, loud and strong.
Green is for a coat, warm and thick.
Green is for a helmet, hard as a stick.
Green is for a crocodile, snappy and brave.
Green is for a tortoise, who lives in a cave.
Green is for a map that is green and blue.
Green is for a ball, bouncy and new.
Green is for a tyrannosaurus, bigger and louder.
Green is for paint, made out of powder and water.
Green is for a book made from card and paint.
Green is for a traffic light, when it changes it faints.
Green is for leaves that are small.
Green is for a soldier's uniform, thin and tall.

Zeeshan Syed (9)
Shaftesbury Primary School

MOTHER'S DAY POEM

Thank you for being a good cook,
And for getting me a book.
Thank you for being kind and nice,
And the way you make rice.
Thank you for making me popcorn.
And for treating me nicely when I was born.
Thank you for reading to me.
And thank you for not making me eat a bumble bee.

Sabba Rashid (8)
Shaftesbury Primary School

THE CALENDAR POEM

January is so cold,
That you could make a snow mould.
February is when the wind will blow,
That would blow away all the snow
March is a time when the rain comes down,
When you can hear a pitter-patter sound.
April is a fun-filled time
That is why I chose this rhyme.
May is when the flowers bloom,
It will be summer soon.
June is very hot,
It feels like I'm in a frying pot.
July is when the sun really shines,
I feel so hot I could draw lots of lines.
August is when my birthday comes,
It seems like I have some funds.
September is not cold, it's chilly,
Even though my dress is frilly.
October is when my brother was born,
And also when my dress was torn.
November is when the leaves really fall,
This tree seems to be extra tall.
December is when your feet start to freeze,
And everybody starts to sneeze.

Karen Johnson (8)
Shaftesbury Primary School

COLOURS

Green is for grass
That is green and strong.
Green is for frogs
That cannot sing a song.
Green is for crocodiles
That are big and long
Green is for trees
That are tall and strong
Green is for a tortoise
Small and strong
Green is for a dragon
Strong and long
Green is for Dipsy
Who is tall and long.

Leona Campbell (8)
Shaftesbury Primary School

FASTER THAN

Faster than a cheetah chasing a deer.
Faster than 100 girls running home.
Faster than 90 boys running to school.
Faster than a police car chasing a robber.
Faster than a car going *zoom* on the motorway.
Faster than a whale swimming to a boat.
Faster than a kite going to the sky.
Faster than 20 lions running to the zoo.
Faster than 30 boys getting chased.
Faster than an aeroplane going to India.

Tayub Nisar (9)
Shaftesbury Primary School

DON'T

Don't hit your brother
Don't kick the cat.
Don't muddy your fingers
Don't sit like that.

Don't fight with your sister
Don't cut off my hair.
Don't eat the goldfish
Don't chase that bear.

Don't rip your book
Don't jump on your sister.
Don't break my hand
Don't cut off my blister.

Don't cut my flowers
Don't scare the cat.
Don't pull my hair
Don't hit Pat.

Don't nick my money
Don't lick the bin.
Don't take my basket
Don't kick the tin.

Alia Adam (10)
Shaftesbury Primary School

DON'T

Don't be a pig
Don't rip the pencil case
Don't eat the pencil
Don't play with that base.

Don't hit your brother
Don't pick your nose
Don't pull the curtains
Don't bite your toes.

Don't be silly
Don't go near the fire
Don't do that
Don't be a liar.

Reshma Halai (9)
Shaftesbury Primary School

GROWLING THE DRAGON

Growling the dragon
Is a kind, kind dragon.
Caroline found him
And brought him home.
She fed him on meat
He said, 'That's sweet.'

He went in a puddle.
Oh what a muddle.
He got so dirty
And became quite shirty
But Caroline bathed him
So Caroline saved him.

Caroline Reilly (8)
Shaftesbury Primary School

SUNNY DAY

Sitting in my back garden wondering what to do,
surrounded by lovely sights and beautiful flowers too.
I'm much too lazy to rise and run,
so I sit back and glance at the sun.
The birds are singing high in the sky.
The sun is shining very bright.
Oh what a beautiful summer's day.

Bharat Halai (9)
Shaftesbury Primary School

WATERFALLS

Water is nice
Water is sparkling
Water is shining
Water is the best!

We use water when we have a bath
We use water when we drink
When it's raining there is water
We all cannot live without water.

Water is tasty!

Hazera Begum (9)
Shaftesbury Primary School

MONEY

The people I could meet with it.
The things that I could buy with it.
Money, I love that stuff.
The people that I could help with it.
The things that I could see with it.
Money, I love that stuff.
The lives that are lost for it.
People who are killed for it
Money, I hate that stuff.

Sunniya Mehmood (10)
Shaftesbury Primary School

THE FUN TIMES

My times is Claire
and I have curly hair.

I play in the sun,
And I have great fun.

I have a cat who
is called Pat

I had a big spider
who was called Cider.

Claire Hastings (9)
Storey Primary School

DOLPHINS SING AND DANCE ALL NIGHT LONG

Dolphins sing and dance all night long,
Always singing a happy song.
I hope that they will sing forever
In all kinds of different weather.
I hope they will never die.
If they do I will cry.

Chantelle Drabble (10)
Storey Primary School

DINOSAURS

Dinosaurs lived long ago
When the earth was covered in snow
They would eat everything in sight
In the morning and in the night
Now you see them in museums
Buy a ticket and go and see 'em.

Peter Akinfenwa (9)
Storey Primary School

FIVE LIVES

My cat's name is Dolly
She only has five lives
I hope she lives forever
And never, never dies.
I feed her every morning
Before I go to school
She is a very clever cat,
And really, really cool.

Liam Cesay (8)
Storey Primary School

SUNLIGHT

The sun is bright
And gives us light.

The sun is hot
And I like it a lot.

The sun is bad when
I am sad.

But when the sun is glad
I am a good lad.

Michael Parrish (10)
Storey Primary School

MY COUSIN JESSICA

My cousin Jessica had a black dress
She went to sit down and sat in a mess.

There was a man who lived next door
And he did break dancing on the floor.

Jessica went into the snow and
                            away we go.

Lee-Ann Folagbade (10)
Storey Primary School

LIFE OR DEATH

Born on Sunday, in London
Hospital.

Had injection on Monday.
Cried out loud.

Home on Tuesday. Mum went
To work.

Argued on Wednesday with Dad.
Left the house never to be
Seen again.

Grew up in a hut on
Thursday and worked until her
Hair was gone.

Captured on Friday . . . into
Slavery and starvation.

Died on Saturday and
Buried in the afternoon.

Egwolo Ekregbesi
Storey Primary School

MY HAMSTER

My hamster's name is Linford
He likes to run around.
He jumped right off the ground.
I tried to pick him up
but he jumped right out of
               my hands.

Christina Head (10)
Storey Primary School

ANTHONY'S WEEK

On Monday
I go to Savecentre

On Tuesday
I go to Arc in the park

On Wednesday
I go to Newhan General Hospital

On Thursday
I go on the Docklands Light Railway

On Friday
I go on the 300 bus to East Ham

On Saturday
I go shopping with Ricky

On Sunday
I stay at home.

Anthony McCarthy (10)
Storey Primary School

TOASTER

My name is Alan
I live in a toaster
My mum said that
I'm a bit of a boaster.

Football is my life
And that's the way it is
Cheryl's to be my wife
Life is such a whiz.

Alan Sanders (9)
Storey Primary School

WINTER

W indy wet weather all day long.
I cicles are hanging down like fingers.
N asty numb necks on a cold day.
T orrential rain with a thundering thunderstorm.
E vergreens give us happiness forever
R eindeer running really fast through
                the wretched rain.

Deborah Anderson (10)
Storey Primary School

ABOUT RICHARD

My name is Richard
I live in East Ham
When I grow up I'll be a man.
I go to school at Storey Street
And my mum said I have
                very smelly feet.
I do my work as best I can
Because when I grow up
                I'll be a man.

Richard Henry (10)
Storey Primary School

HOW STEVENA HARWOOD GREW UP

Born on a Thursday
Lovely and chubby

Her eyes sparkle
So shiny and bright

Her hair lovely
Shiny and silky

When she was one
She said 'Mummy, potty'

When she was three
She climbed a tree

When she was five
She wanted to drive

When she was seven
She went to Devon

When she was nine
She loved to be kind

Now she is ten,
She's been to see Big Ben.

Stacey Donaldson (9)
Storey Primary School

My Nan

I was born on a Monday
Safe and sound.

I was diagnosed on a Tuesday
In the hospital.

I was sick on a Wednesday
Very bad.

Went into hospital on a Thursday
They tried to make me better
But no hope.

Died on a Friday
In peace.

Buried on a Saturday
Ready for another life

Mum and Dad crying on a Sunday.
Upset everyone.

Carol Hastings (9)
Storey Primary School

COSMIC

As I rocketed through the stars,
I spotted Mercury, Venus, then Mars.
When I flew past Uranus I saw,
A huge, giant, meteor,
I tried to swerve, oh how I tried!
And as I did it, almost died.
Although, thank God I did not,
Then something said 'Oh that's hot!'
Then I shouted 'Who said that?'
And there I saw a wonderful cat.
'How did you get into my craft?'
'Through the door' he said, and laughed.
'I've got a ship as well,' he said,
'It's really cool - and made of lead.
Could I come to your planet - Earth?
I've wanted to since my birth.'
Suddenly I woke up and said,
'Damn, I was enjoying that dream
                in my comfortable bed.'
'What was it about?' said my wonderful cat,
So I told him about it, and that was that.

Alexander Richards (10)
Wellington Primary School

COSMIC STARS

C an you see the universe?
O r can you see a UFO?
S tars are nice stars are bright
M ars is red so is my friend
I n space you can see the Milky Way
C ome to space it's a lovely place.

Marc White (10)
Wellington Primary School

THE STAR

On a dark, cold night
people say that the stars shine bright
and they are right
because I have seen them and it is
                a wonderful sight.

I look at the sky every night
but what I see is never seen in light
because when the sky is white
you cannot see this wonderful sight.

I shall never forget what is special about the night
I shall never forget the things that shine bright
I shall never forget
        This wonderful sight!

Daniella Hussein (11)
Wellington Primary School

COSMIC

If I could see the moon tonight,
I'm sure that it is very bright.
Either way, I'm going out of my mind
All the answers to my questions,
I have to find.
Is the sun as hot as lava?
Is the moon made of cheese?
Are the stars colder than lava,
Or are they all the same?
Does Santa Claus live in a star?
Is there such a thing as God?
Either way, I have to know.

Natalie Chalmers (11)
Wellington Primary School

Cosmic

Cosmic, cosmic, why can cosmic be so fast?
Faster than a jet aircraft,
But what I can't get is,
How can it be faster than
A Concorde, jet aircraft?

Cosmic, cosmic, why is space so dark?
Is it because it's bad?
Why is it so dark up there?
Do they paint the sky black every year?

There's something coming,
From a place called space,
But I hope there's a bit of space for me up there,
For me to put my space figures up there,
Until my room has got more space.

Tony Braddick (11)
Wellington Primary School

Cosmic Stuff

I went to space,
It was a lovely place
I had a good time, really.

I don't know why, to tell you the truth,
I'd rather be playing out with Ruth!

Ruth's my best friend,
She's really cool
But sometimes she can be a bit of a fool!
Am I being horrible?
If so, I want to know!

Louise Britton (10)
Wellington Primary School

UFOs

Sudden glimmer,
Sudden flash.
Then the beam
Then a crash
Twinkling light
Into the ship
Can hear the sound
Of a paper clip
All the way out of the atmosphere
Looking out of the window
Seeing the country roads disappear
In the distance of the ship
The ET talking on the telephone
And me saying
      'ET phone home.'

Darryl Neal (11)
Wellington Primary School

IF I GO TO THE STAR

If I could - I would go to a star.
I'd fly by rocket.
It would take some years.
Maybe I'd find aliens.

Maybe he'd say
'If you come with me,
I'll give you a chocolate
Mars bar and I might go with him.'

Nefise Dervish (9)
Wellington Primary School

EARTH VISIT

He landed here on Earth one day,
He was from a galaxy far away.

He spoke not a word, but went straight to his work,
To see what civilisation's like here on Earth.

He wore a blue coat,
And was green in the face.

I knew in a moment,
He was from outer space.

When he finished his work,
He gave me a glance,

And I almost went
Into a trance.

Aaron Parvez (11)
Wellington Primary School

PLANET WATCHING

Mercury is sunbathing again
Venus is looking at rockets going past
Earth is playing football
Mars is eating Mars bars
And Jupiter is on a diet
Saturn is playing loop the loop
And Uranus is looking at his moons
Neptune is looking blue
Pluto is freezing cold
Planet Timothy is OK.

Timothy Gibson (10)
Wellington Primary School

COSMIC

I'm writing home
Saying
I'm having a lovely time

I'm on Earth
Flying to Mars
Having a lovely time

I'm in space
Eating cakes
Having a lovely time

I fell off Mars
Landed on the stars
Having a lovely time

I will not be
Coming home, but
Having a lovely time

I will not be
Coming home, but
Having a lovely time

Lots of Love
Kate
Having a lovely time.

Kate Newby (10)
Wellington Primary School

BRIGHT NIGHT!

Bright night,
Bright night
You brighten up my life tonight.

Bright night,
Bright night
I love that star tonight.

Bright night,
Bright night
Fly away, that star tonight.

Bright night,
Bright night
I just want to say goodbye and good night.

Bright night,
Bright night
Let that star shine bright tonight.

Aimée Swallow (11)
Wellington Primary School

PLANETS AND STARS

I went to Mars to see all the stars.
I stayed overnight to view the sights.

I travelled to each planet to find my cousin Janet.
She wasn't anywhere,
But I didn't really care.

I went to the sun - originally for fun.
But whilst I was there,
I lost all my hair.

I went to Saturn to learn some Latin.
I didn't learn much but I speak
                              Double Dutch!

Charlotte Barrett (10)
Wellington Primary School

CLASS TOPSY TURVY

There's a fish tank in our class, no fish
There's a guinea-pig cage in our class, no guinea-pig
And as far as our teachers are concerned
There's children's skulls with no brains in them.
Mind you though the only thing that's full to the brim
Is the waste paper bin!
Outside the houses of the class children
Bang, crash, rattle, tat
Oh my gosh what was that?
It came from outside maybe I'd better hide
A few hours later everyone's asleep
Zitoo, zitoo, zitoo, bleep
In comes the alien with a few alien brains.
Oh what's happened? The children are insane
Someone's given them alien brains!
I 'ave always 'ated deez teechirs
Children sit down
But promiz not to hurt uz!
Gurgle, gurgle, gurgle, plop
The alien goes back to planet Zot!

Spencer Bain (10)
Wellington Primary School

Cosmic

There was a huge crash,
That made a bang,
I sprang from my bed,
And something had fallen down.
A flying saucer!
Had fallen from the sky,
It had bright lights,
That came tumbling by.
An alien came with lovely eyes
Came up to my window,
And tapped on the glass.
I jumped with fright,
Made an amazing leap,
Flew out of the window,
And landed in a huge heap.
The alien came,
Pointed a finger,
As he did so I began to quiver.
Flashing green lights,
Dazzled my eyes.
The flying saucer
Was a UFO,
This means unexplained fake object
If you want to know!

Hayley White (11)
Wellington Primary School

ONCE I WAS...

Once I was an alien flying in the sky
Going down below saying 'Hi! Hi! Hi!'

Now I am a star, bright in the dark,
Wishing I had wings just like a lark.

Once I was the Milky Way going round in rings
Looking at the bay, and other lovely things.

Now I'm like a pencil sitting in the pot,
Looking round among my friends feeling very hot!

Once I was an astronaut flying to the moon,
Now I am an alien visiting space very soon.

Daniel Burt (10)
Wellington Primary School

THE CREATURE

Out in the Cosmos,
The final frontier,
Lurks a creature,
None can hear.

It can take the form
Of anything,
So be careful,
it might suck you in.

No one knows, where it comes from,
Or what it seeks,
But we know it can
look like
Anything.

Shakeel Sanghera (10)
Wellington Primary School

MY SPACE MOUSE

I had a space mouse
Who lived in a space house.
He saw a star
But it wasn't very far.

I went to Mars
To find the stars.
But saw the moon
It came too soon.

My mouse came from space.
He hated that place.
I returned him to Mars
To eat chocolate bars.

Karen Tapp (10)
Wellington Primary School

MY VISIT TO MARS

I was going to stay on Jupiter,
But decided to visit Mars,
I like to see the milky stars,
And watch them twinkling from afar.
On Tuesday I saw my alien friend,
I found his brother at his wit's end.
On Wednesday I returned to Mars,
To watch the silver shiny stars.
On Thursday night I had a fright,
But decided to stay one more night.
On Friday I went back to Earth again,
Now I won't see anymore
Spacemen!

Hannah Bartlett (9)
Wellington Primary School

I'M GOING INTO SPACE

I'm going into space,
It's my first time in that big place.
I saw a cow which went *miaow*.
I got to my rocket with my hands in my pocket.
I landed on Mars and ate my choco bars.
I turned around and did a triple jump
Then I remembered my mega pump!
I pumped myself up, till I burst!
I joined a race and I came first.
I decided to come down,
It was too boring up there.
When I came through the clouds
I floated on air.

Terry Oliver (9)
Wellington Primary School

COSMIC SPACE

In the stars right by Mars
I eat a Mars bar,
I packed another,
Only to discover
It was a Milky Way.

I jumped into the shuttle 54321
Blast off! There I was in the stars
Waving goodbye to Mars.

I was in the shuttle,
It made a ruttle on my way home
I was sad but I was glad
That I was safely home.

Bo Lauezzari (10)
Wellington Primary School

POETRY IN MARS

Once I went to Mars
I could only see the stars.
I was once in space
I was looking for a place.
Thinking of somewhere
Such a wonderful place.
I wanted to stay around in space,
But I couldn't find the right place.

My mum asked me to stay,
So I looked for a way,
To return to the place
Somewhere in space.

I found my home
Without having to roam,
It's a massive place,
Bright and full of grace.

Mickayla Brown (10)
Wellington Primary School

MY FIRST TIME IN SPACE

It was my first time in space,
Oh! What a lovely place.
I was up in Mars,
And I saw some stars.
I stayed all night,
'Cos it was a wonderful sight.
My rocket went zoom,
It crashed and went boom!
I didn't really care,
For I had one more spare.

I had an alien friend,
Which started a trend.
Zoog lived in Jupiter,
His mum was called Cupiter.
We loved to play,
All through the day.
When he got mean,
He went all green.
Sometimes he was fun,
Till he pulled out a gun.
We went to the moon,
In a massive cocoon.
Then I went back home,
And all I did was moan.

Holly Sterling (10)
Wellington Primary School

SPACE AND PLANETS

On my way to Mars,
I met all the superstars.
They had the best chocolate bars.

I wish I went to Saturn,
It twirls and makes a pattern.

I wish I went to Pluto,
To play the game Subbuteo.

I wish I could go to planet X,
To see if there are jumbo jets.

I wish I could go to the sun,
To eat some food and have some fun.

I wish I could go to the moon,
And live like a butterfly in a cocoon.

I wish I could go to Venus,
Then people would think I am a genius.

Elysseos Odesseos (10)
Wellington Primary School

SOLAR SYSTEM

I was really happy
when I won the race,
because the prize was
a trip to space.

I've never seen Mars before,
just the stars and
no more.

Mercury's hot and
Pluto's cool,
If you land on the sun
You're a fool!

Meteors fly everywhere,
It's hard to dodge them
up in the air.

I'd like to see an alien,
because they speak
Australian.

When I went to the moon,
I found a card saying
'See you soon.'

When I went around Saturn,
I saw the snowflakes
and all their patterns.

Kieran Street (9)
Wellington Primary School

THE ALIEN

There was an alien from out of space
With a green body and a black and white face.
He came from the planet Bupa Bupa
He said it was great, he said it was super.

He said he didn't like Mars
Because there were no stars.
He hated Jupiter
All people there were stupider.

He said he had to see the rest
But he said Earth was the best.
He said 'Bye bye'
And flew back into the sky.

Two days later I got a letter
From an alien who was sick then got better
To say he was on the planet Sool
And said it was fun, he said it was cool.

He said he had visited the planet Dandy
And bought a lot of things that were very handy
I asked him if he will come back
But he said he made a new friend, Jack.

Samantha Lustig (9)
Wellington Primary School

PLANET HOLIDAY

Would you like to go to the moon?
I hear that was a big shadow of doom.

Miss Miss
Would you like to go to Mars?
I hear that they sell big giant cars.

Miss Miss
Go to space,
Yesterday you told me you needed a bigger place.

Miss Miss
If you go to Mars,
You can see all the big big stars.

Miss Miss
If you go to space,
You could buy a bigger place.

Miss Miss
If you go to Jupiter,
You could get a bigger computer.

Miss Miss
If you go on a rocket,
You could get a bigger locket.

Miss Miss
If you go near the sun,
You could get a big big gun.

Christine Day (9)
Wellington Primary School

SPACE SPACE

Space, space,
I will always see a black case.
I don't know where it comes from,
Inside there might be a song.

Space, space,
Where will I go from here?
Space might give me a beer,
Is it so true just for you,
Can I go round the world and see you too?

Space, space,
What a place.
Can we play a game of chase?
What do I see can it be
A big boot in the sea?

Space, space,
I love to race.
And it looks like a face,
I can see the sun,
While eating a bun.

Karla Thurston (9)
Wellington Primary School

GET TO KNOW SPACE

On Saturn,
People speak Latin,
Which is a language I don't know.

On Earth,
You had your birth,
And lived there all your life.

The moon,
Is like a big baboon,
Except the moon is white and round.

The sun,
Is like a big big bun,
But it's got no icing or currants.

On Mars,
You can see all the stars,
It's a really good view for tourists.

On Jupiter,
It is told astronauts get stupider when they go
To Jupiter,
But I think they were stupid already.

There are a lot more planets than that,
But I need to feed my cat,
Sorry about that!

Lisa Clavey (9)
Wellington Primary School

SPACE THE FINAL FRONTIER

Space the final frontier,
These are the voyages of the star ship Nor,
Who will boldly go where no one has gone before.

Captain's log star space one point two,
We've met an alien with the flu,
She's gone green with pink spots.

Captain's log star space double 0 one,
We are being fired on by a Klingon,
Bang bang bang!

Captain's log star space seven point five,
We're racing past the moon,
He's firing, boom!

Captain's log star space seven, seven, one,
We are passing Mars,
And dodging the stars.

Georgina Whitehead (9)
Wellington Primary School

SPACE

I want to go to Mars,
and watch the lovely stars
Also eat lots of Mars bars.

I'd like to go to the moon,
Too late! It went boom.
I'd wish I got there sooner
Because it was so super.

I want to go to Saturn,
To draw its lovely pattern.
I need to sit down,
In the whole thing I was wearing my gown.

It was really black, so I turned on the light,
I was in a sack.
Where am I
I was in a spaceship oh my!

I got safely home
Oh no I'm in a dome.
My mum came over it's time for bed
So she took me and I asked for butter on bread.

(So that was the last journey in space.)

Kerri-Leigh Jones (10)
Wellington Primary School

ALIENS AND ASTRONAUTS

'Oi alien, which way to the sun?'
'You want to burn your bum?'
'No, which way to the sun, you're a bit dumb.'
'I don't suck my thumb.'
'OK then which way to Mars?'
'I don't eat chocolate bars.'
'No which way to Mars?'
'You want to watch the stars.'
'OK then, where are you going?'
'It's not snowing.'
'No, where are you going!'
'Oh, where am I going?'
'Yes.'
'To Jupiter.'
'Can you take me there then?'

Joel Silverman (10)
Wellington Primary School

FIREWORKS

Fireworks are pretty.
I like indigo.
Rockets exploding into ash.
Excellent fireworks.
Wonderful fireworks.
Orange and red fireworks.
Rolling in the sky.
Kicking in the sky.
Shining in the sky.

Heather Roffey (7)
Whittingham Community Primary School

FIREWORKS!

F ireworks are like a big explosion.
I like them because they make me think of stars.
R olling Catherines glowing in the dark night.
E xciting in the night.
W hat nice colours in the sky.
O range, red and brown.
R ockets up in the sky.
K eys rattling in my ears.
S cattering in the sky.

Stephanie Lashley (8)
Whittingham Community Primary School

FIREWORKS

Fireworks are exploding
In big bangs of lightning.
Roaring like thunder+
Exploding like bombs.
Whooshing like the wind.
On a good day it's exciting.
Rushing like the snow.
Catherine wheels
Spinning like the Earth.

Nathan Onojaife (7)
Whittingham Community Primary School

FOXES

F oxes are red,
O range and brown.
X -ray eyes at night.
E verything in sight, they are
S ly creatures.

Calum Lewis (7)
Whittingham Community Primary School

TIGERS

T igers are very big cats
I think they are great
G o tigers go you're as fast as a car!
E lephants are your prey
R acing through the jungle
S neaking through the grass.

Joe Tollady (7)
Whittingham Community Primary School

WAR AND PEACE

War brings fighting.
Peace brings kindness.
War is bad.
Peace is good.
War brings guns.
Peace brings love.
War and peace.

Hussnain Iqbal (7)
Whittingham Community Primary School

Ms Barry

M s Barry is very beautiful.
S he is a very nice headteacher.
B y day Ms Barry gets sweeter.
A nd has golden hair.
R unning round the school she looks really cool.
R ight and left she runs and never forgets her mums.
Y ou are the best headteacher in the world.

Natalia Robinson (8)
Whittingham Community Primary School

Ms Barry

M s Barry is beautiful.
S he looks after people.
B y day Ms Barry gets sweeter
A nd has very beautiful hair.
R unning round the school looking very cool.
R ight and left she runs never forgets her mums.
Y ou are the best headteacher.

Amy Cantor (7)
Whittingham Community Primary School

Winter Poem

When the winter takes over the autumn.
When the sun has gone in and the kids are locked in.
I hate the winter, please let it be summer again.

Nadine Gore (7)
Whittingham Community Primary School

FIREWORKS

F ireworks are colourful
I like indigo fireworks
R ockets exploding into ash
E xcellent fireworks
W onderful fireworks
O range fireworks
R ockets are colourful
K eys rattling in the air
S ee how colourful they are.

Loren Munroe-Thompson (7)
Whittingham Community Primary School

WINTER POEM

The winter is miserable.
The snow is the deepest, the sun is the weakest.
But the winter's freezing and foggy.
When children are playing with snow and making snowmen.

Michaela Scott (7)
Whittingham Community Primary School

WINTER POEM

It's snowing.
It's freezing.
Snowflakes are falling fast and slow, bright and white to the ground.
Crystal and brightness come from above the sky.
It is cold it is freezing it is snowing outside.

Sahariyea Siddique (8)
Whittingham Community Primary School

WINTER POEM

Autumn is gone winter has started,
All the people are cold-hearted,
Hang up decorations on the Christmas trees,
All the animals are hiding, including the bees.
People are making snowmen.
All the doves have gone in their den.
The leaves are not falling.
The birds are not calling.

Zoyyah Imran (8)
Whittingham Community Primary School

WINTER POEM

Today it is very wintry.
I am freezing.
I am playing in the snow.

Tony Bradfield (7)
Whittingham Community Primary School

WINTER POEM

The night is the coldest.
The water is deep.
Freezing, it turns to ice.
People hate to fall.
The ice is hard.
But sometimes I am shivering.
The wind is blowing because the winter is calling.

Kyle Clarke (7)
Whittingham Community Primary School

WINTER POEM

I hate winter.
No sun,
No fun,
Just miserable and cold.
The snow is deep
And sharp.
The wind is hard,
And foggy, freezing and cold.

Ruebin Forbes (8)
Whittingham Community Primary School